C000184331

Off-road routes

First published 1997 by

Ordnance Survey and George Philip Ltd, an imprint of
Romsey Road   Reed Books
Maybush   Michelin House
Southampton   81 Fulham Road
SO16 4GU   London SW3 6RB

Text and compilation
Copyright © Reed International Books Ltd 1997
Maps Copyright © Crown Copyright 1997

**The route maps in this book are based upon
Ordnance Survey® Landranger® mapping.**

**The cross-profile diagrams in this book have
been created using Ordnance Survey®
Land-Form PANORAMA™ Digital height data.**

Ordnance Survey and Landranger are registered trade
marks and Land-Form PANORAMA is a trade mark of
Ordnance Survey, the National Mapping Agency of
Great Britain.

First edition 1997

A catalogue record for this atlas is available from the
British Library

ISBN 0 600 59105 0
Printed in Spain

Acknowledgements
AA Photo Library 37, 49, 55, 61, 67, 97, 111, 115, 119, 123, 127, 139
Joe Cornish 17, 73, 79 • Derek Forss 131 • Leslie Garland Picture Library
(Leslie Garland) 107, (Phil Nixon) 103 • David Tarn back cover, 29, 43
Jim Winkley 23, 85, 91.

• edited by Melissa Arnison-Newgass • designed by Ian Muggeridge
• picture research by Jenny Faithfull • production by Claudette Morris
• art editor: James Hughes

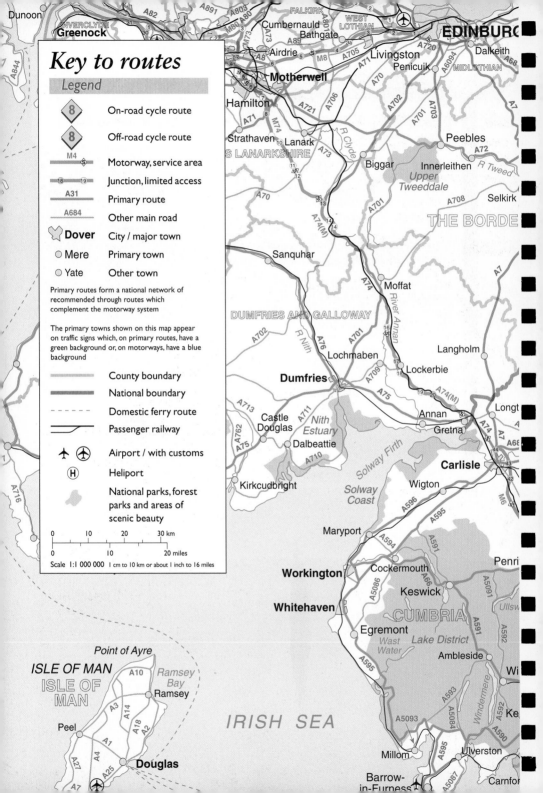

Ordnance Survey

Cycle

TOURS

24 one-day routes in

Northumberland and County Durham

Compiled by
Ted Liddle

PHILIP'S

Contents

On-road routes

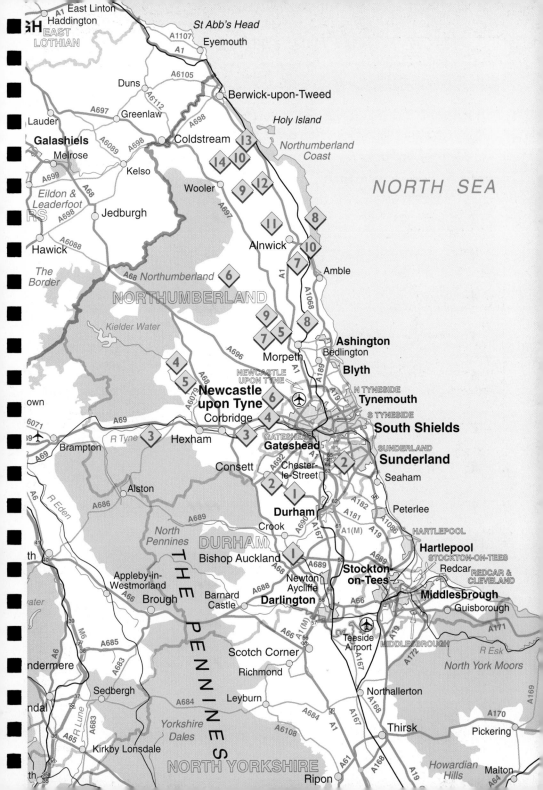

Quick reference chart

Route	Page	Distance (kilometres)	Grade (easy/moderate/ strenuous)	Links with other routes[1]	Tourist information centres[2]
On-road routes					
1 West from Durham City into the Deerness Valley	16	54	🚲🚲🚲 🚲🚲🚲🚲	2	Durham 0191 384 3720
2 The Consett and Sunderland railway path and Lanchester Valley	22	42/29	🚲	1	Beamish 0191 370 2533
3 Along the Tyne Valley from Haltwhistle	28	69	🚲🚲		Haltwhistle 01434 322002
4 From Stocksfield, to the north and south of the Tyne Valley	36	63/45	🚲🚲 🚲🚲🚲	6	Prudhoe 01661 833144
5 The north Tyne Valley, east of Bellingham and west of Wark	42	62/45	🚲🚲🚲🚲		Bellingham 01434 220616
6 Northwest of Ponteland, along quiet roads to Capheaton	48	56	🚲🚲	4,7	Newcastle-upon-Tyne 0191 261 0691
7 Westward to Wallington from Morpeth of Mitford	54	67	🚲🚲🚲	6,8,9	Morpeth 01670 511323
8 Northeast of Morpeth to Cresswell on the coast	60	43/25	🚲	7,9	Morpeth 01670 511323
9 Northwest of Morpeth to Rothbury, returning via The Fords	66	73/52	🚲🚲🚲🚲	7,8	Morpeth 01670 511323
10 A coastal circuit from Alnwick via Warkworth and Alnmouth	72	59/35	🚲🚲🚲	11	Alnwick 01665 510665
11 West of Alnwick, through the Vale of Whittingham	78	67/46	🚲🚲🚲	10	Alnwick 01665 510665
12 From Belford to Seahouses, returning over Chatton Moor	84	55	🚲🚲🚲	13	Seahouses 01665 720884
13 A circuit of the Kyloe Hills and a visit to Holy Island	90	48	🚲	12,14	Wooler 01668 81602

Route	Page	Distance (kilometres)	Grade (easy/moderate/strenuous)	Links with other routes[1]	Tourist information centres[2]
14 North of Wooler to the Scottish Border, returning by Ford and Etal	96	66/44 🚲🚲		13	Wooler 01668 81602

Off-road routes

Route	Page	Distance (kilometres)	Grade (easy/moderate/strenuous)	Links with other routes[1]	Tourist information centres[2]
1 A circuit from Bishop Auckland on railway paths and quiet lanes	102	29 🚲			Durham 0191 384 3720
2 East of Washington, around Penshaw Monument	106	22 🚲			Sunderland 0191 565 0960/0990
3 Along the Tyne from Prudhoe then southwest from Wylam	110	39/25 🚲🚲🚲 🚲🚲🚲🚲			Prudhoe 01661 833144
4 Across fells north of Bellingham and east to Linnheads Lake	114	42/24 🚲🚲🚲🚲 🚲🚲🚲🚲🚲			Bellingham 01434 220616
5 Weaving along the Wansbeck, west of Morpeth	118	46 🚲🚲			Morpeth 01670 511323
6 The Rothbury Round	122	44/25 🚲🚲🚲🚲 🚲🚲🚲🚲🚲			Rothbury 01669 20887
7 South of Alnwick to the coast as far as Warkworth	126	43/32 🚲	8		Alnwick 01665 510665
8 East of Alnwick to the coast, north to Craster	130	34/32 🚲 🚲🚲	7		Alnwick 01665 510665
9 A super circuit on scenic byways, south of Wooler	134	34/20 🚲🚲🚲			Wooler 01668 81602
10 West of Belford to St Cuthbert's Cave and Ravens Crag	138	21/18 🚲			Wooler 01668 81602

[1]**Links with other routes** Use this information to create a more strenuous ride or if you are planning to do more than one ride in a day or on a weekend or over a few days. The rides do not necessarily join: there may be a distance of about 5 km (3 miles) between the closest points. Several rides are in pairs, sharing the same starting point, which may be a good place to base yourself for a weekend.

[2]**Tourist Information Centres** You can contact them for details about accommodation. If they cannot help, there are many books that recommend places to stay. If nothing is listed for the place where you want to stay, try phoning the post office or the pub in the village to see if they can suggest somewhere.

Northumberland and County Durham

Northumberland is one of the most beautiful counties in England with its wonderfully diverse range of landscapes and fascinating historical links. County Durham has its own personality and it too has an abundance of un-crowded roads which meander through unspoilt countryside. Both counties are richly blessed with a combination of wide open spaces and a labyrinthine network of quiet roads; even the conurbations in Tyne and Wear can boast an ever-growing network of bike-friendly narrow lanes and cycle paths. The region's four principal rivers, the Tweed, Tyne, Wear and Tees all pass through outstanding scenery on their way to the sea and together they provide inspiration, as well as natural boundaries, for the cycle tours contained in this book. One of the cleanest and most attractive coastlines in England supplies the eastern limit and such is the amazing array of possible cycle tours that only routes lying to the east of the North Pennines and the Cheviot Hills have been chosen for this volume.

Five main bases cover most of the tours; Durham City serves several routes, although more localised starting points are described. Morpeth, Alnwick, Belford and Wooler are the principal centres in Northumberland most of which give ready access to the coast with its castles and islands as well as splendid inland tours. Rothbury also features as does both the North and South Tyne Valleys; the linear route between Newcastle and Haltwistle is modelled on the National Cycle Network route to Hadrian's Wall country. Only the coastal routes, the railway paths and the eastern half of the Tyne Valley are level; there are numerous uphill sections to climb up out of the region's many valleys but that does mean that there are some wonderful descents! A reasonable level of fitness will mean that you will be able to tackle and enjoy every route in this book but there are quite a few routes which you can do to make the process of getting fit highly pleasurable. Many of the on-road routes follow wonderfully quiet country roads; off-road routes are never totally off-road but share a mixture of forgotten byways, hidden-away tracks and traffic-free railway paths thus making route selection a delight.

This truly is 'the secret corner of England' and it is likely to remain so for some considerable time even though guides like this are revealing some of its best kept secrets to an ever-growing number of cyclists.

Abbreviations and instructions

Instructions are given as concisely as possible to make them easy to follow while you are cycling. Remember to read one or two instructions ahead so that you do not miss a turning. This is most likely to occur when you have to turn off a road on which you have been riding for a fairly long distance and these junctions are marked **Easy to miss** to warn you.

If there appears to be a contradiction between the instructions and what you actually see, always refer to the map. There are many reasons why over the course of a few years instructions will need updating as new roads are built and priorities and signposts change.

If giving instructions for road routes is at times difficult, doing so for off-road routes can often be almost impossible, particularly when the route passes through woodland. With few signposts and buildings by which to orientate yourself, more attention is paid to other features, such as gradient and surface. Most of these routes have been explored between late spring and early autumn and the countryside changes its appearance very dramatically in winter. If in doubt, consult your map and check your compass to see that you are heading in the right direction.

Where I have encountered mud I have mentioned it, but this may change, not only from summer to winter but also from dry to wet weather, at any time during the year. At times you may have to retrace your steps and find a road alternative.

Some routes have small sections that follow footpaths. The instructions will highlight these sections where you must get off and push your bike. You may only ride on bridleways and by-ways so be careful if you stray from the given routes.

Directions

L	left
LH	left-hand
RH	right-hand
SA	straight ahead or straight across
bear L or R	make less than a 90-degree (right-angle) turn at a fork in the road or track or at a sharp bend so that your course appears to be straight ahead; this is often written as *in effect SA*
sharp L or R turn	is more acute than 90 degrees
sharp R/L back on yourself	an almost U-turn
sharp LH/RH bend	a 90-degree bend
R then L or R	the second turning is visible then immediately L from the first
R then 1st L	the second turning may be some distance from the first; the distance may also be indicated: *R, then after 1 mile L*

Junctions

T-j	T-junction, a junction where you have to give way
X-roads	crossroads, a junction where you may or may not have to give way
offset X-roads	the four roads are not in the form of a perfect cross and you will have to turn left then right, or vice versa, to continue the route

Signs

'Placename 2'	words in quotation marks are those that appear on signposts; the numbers indicate distance in miles unless stated otherwise
NS	not signposted
trig point	a trigonometrical station

Instructions

An example of an easy instruction is:

4 At the T-j at the end of Smith Road by the White Swan PH R on Brown Street 'Greentown 2, Redville 3'.

There is more information in this instruction than you would normally need, but things do change: pubs may close down and signs may be replaced, removed or vandalized.

An example of a difficult instruction is:

8 Shortly after the brow of the hill, soon after passing a telephone box on the right next L (NS).

As you can see, there is no T-junction to halt you in your tracks, no signpost indicating where the left turn will take you, so you need to have your wits about you in order not to miss the turning.

Fact boxes

The introduction to each route includes a fact box giving useful information:

Start

This is the suggested start point coinciding with instruction 1 on the map. There is no reason why you should not start at another point if you prefer.

Distance and grade

The distance is, of course, that from the beginning to the end of the route. If you wish to shorten the ride, however, the maps enable you to do so.

The number of drinks bottles indicates the grade:
Easy
Moderate
Strenuous

Page diagrams

The on-road routes usually occupy four pages of mapping each. The page diagrams on the introductory pages show how the map pages have been laid out, how they overlap and if any inset maps have been used.

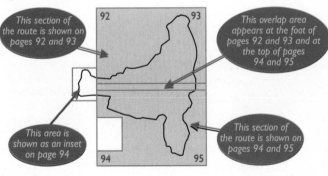

This section of the route is shown on pages 92 and 93

This overlap area appears at the foot of pages 92 and 93 and at the top of pages 94 and 95

This area is shown as an inset on page 94

This section of the route is shown on pages 94 and 95

The grade is based on the amount of climbing involved.

Remember that conditions may vary dramatically with the weather and seasons, especially along off-road sections

Terrain

This brief description of the terrain may be read in conjunction with the cross-profile diagram at the foot of the page to help you to plan your journey.

Nearest railway

This is the distance to the nearest station from the closest point on the route, not necessarily from the start. Before starting out you should check with British Rail for local restrictions regarding the carrying of bicycles.

Refreshments

Pubs and teashops on or near the route are listed. The tankard symbols indicate pubs particularly liked by the author.

Before you go

Preparing yourself

Fitness

Cycling uses muscles in a different way from walking or running, so if you are beginning or returning to it after a long absence you will need time to train your muscles and become accustomed to sitting on a saddle for a few hours. Build up your fitness and stamina gradually and make sure you are using a bicycle that is the right size for you and suits your needs.

Equipment

Attach the following items to the bike: bell, pump, light-brackets and lights, lock-holder and lock, rack and panniers or elastic straps for securing things to the rack, map holder. Unless it is the middle of summer and the weather is guaranteed to be fine, you will need to carry extra clothes, particularly a waterproof, with you, and it is well worth investing in a rack for this purpose.

Wearing a small pouch around your waist is the easiest and safest way of carrying small tools and personal equipment. The basics are: Allen keys to fit the various Allen bolts on your bike, chainlink extractor, puncture repair kit, reversible screwdriver (slot and crosshead), small adjustable spanner, spare inner tube, tyre levers (not always necessary with mountain bike tyres), coins and a phonecard for food and telephone calls, compass.

Additional tools for extended touring: bottom bracket extractor, cone spanners, freewheel extractor, headset spanners, lubricant, socket spanner for pedals, spare cables, spoke-key.

Clothing

What you wear when you are cycling should be comfortable, allowing you, and most especially your legs, to move freely. It should also be practical, so that it will keep you warm and dry if and when the weather changes.

Feet You can cycle in just about any sort of footwear, but bear in mind that the chain has oil on it, so do not use your very best shoes. Leather tennis shoes or something similar, with a smooth sole to slip into the pedal and toe clip are probably adequate until you buy specialist cycling shoes, which have stiffer soles and are sometimes designed for use with specialist pedals.

Legs Cycling shorts or padded cycling underwear worn under everyday clothing make long rides much more comfortable. Avoid tight, non-stretch trousers, which are very uncomfortable for cycling and will sap your energy, as they restrict the movement of your legs; baggy tracksuit bottoms, which can get caught in the chain and will sag around your ankles if they get wet. Almost anything else will do, though a pair of stretch leggings is probably best.

Upper body What you wear should be long enough to cover your lower back when you are leaning forward and, ideally, should have zips or buttons that you can adjust to regulate your temperature. Several thin layers are better than one thick layer.

Head A helmet may protect your head in a fall.

Wet weather A waterproof, windproof top is essential if it looks like rain. A dustbin bag would be better than nothing but obviously a breathable waterproof material is best.

Cold weather A hat that covers your ears, a scarf around your neck, a pair of warm gloves and a thermal top and bottom combined with what you would normally wear cycling should cover almost all conditions.

Night and poor light Wearing light-coloured clothes or reflective strips is almost as important as having lights on your bike. Reflective bands worn around the ankles are particularly effective in making you visible to motorists.

Preparing your bicycle

You may not be a bicycle maintenance expert, but you should make sure that your bike is roadworthy before you begin a ride.

If you are planning to ride in soft, off-road conditions, fit fat, knobbly tyres. If you are using the bike around town or on a road route, fit narrower, smoother tyres.

Check the tyres for punctures or damage and repair or replace if necessary or if you are in any doubt. Keep tyres inflated hard (recommended pressures are on the side wall of the tyre) for mainly on-road riding. You do not need to inflate tyres as hard for off-road use; slightly softer tyres give some cushioning and get better traction in muddy conditions.

Ensure that the brakes work efficiently. Replace worn cables and brake blocks.

The bike should glide along silently. Tighten and adjust any part that is loose or rubbing against a moving part. Using a good-quality bike oil lubricate the hubs, bottom bracket, pedals where they join the cranks, chain and gear-changing mechanism from both sides. If the bike still makes grating noises, replace the bearings.

Adjust the saddle properly. The saddle height should ensure that your legs are working efficiently: too low and your knees will ache; too high and your hips will be rocking in order for your feet to reach the pedals. Some women find the average bike saddle uncomfortable because the female pelvis is a different shape from the male pelvis and needs a broader saddle for support. Some manufacturers make saddles especially for women.

Cross-profiles

The introduction to each route includes a cross-profile diagram. The blue grid indicates 1-kilometre horizontal intervals and 50-metre vertical intervals

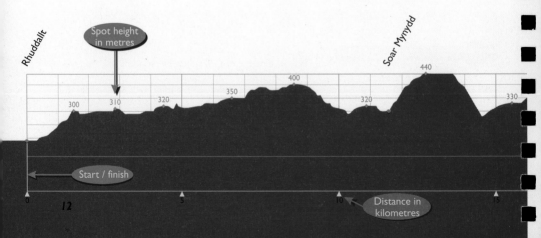

12

Transporting your bike

There are three ways of getting you and your bike to the start of a ride:

- **Cycle** to the start or to a point along a route
- **Take the train.** Always check in advance that you can take the bike on the train. Some trains allow only up to two bikes and you may need to make a reservation and pay a flat fee however long the journey. Always label your bike showing your name and destination station.
- **By motor vehicle.** You can carry the bikes:

  Inside the vehicle. Many bikes have quick-release mechanisms on both wheels and the seatpost, which allow a quick dismantling of the bike to fit in even quite small cars.

  On top of the vehicle. The advantages of this method are that the bikes are completely out of the way and are not resting against each other, you can get at the boot or hatch easily and the bikes do not obscure the number plate or rear lights and indicators.

  On a rack that attaches to the rear of the vehicle. The advantages are that the rack and bikes are easily accessible, also fuel consumption is better than with a roof-rack.

Code of Conduct

- Enjoy the countryside and respect its life and work
- Only ride where you know you have a legal right
- Always yield to horses and pedestrians
- Take all litter with you
- Don't get annoyed with anyone; it never solves any problems
- Guard against all risk of fire
- Fasten all gates
- Keep your dogs under close control
- Keep to public paths across farmland
- Use gates and stiles to cross fences, hedges and walls
- Avoid livestock, crops and machinery or, if not possible, keep contact to a minimum
- Help keep all water clean
- Protect wildlife, plants and trees
- Take special care on country roads
- Make no unnecessary noise

Whichever way you carry the bikes on the outside of the vehicle, ensure that you regularly check that they are secure and that straps and fixings that hold them in place have not come loose. If you are leaving the bikes for any length of time, be sure they are secure against theft; if nothing else lock them to each other.

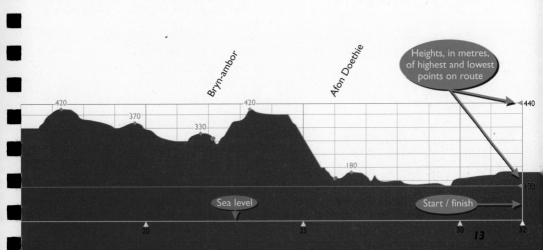

Legend to 1:50 000 maps

Roads and paths

Motorway

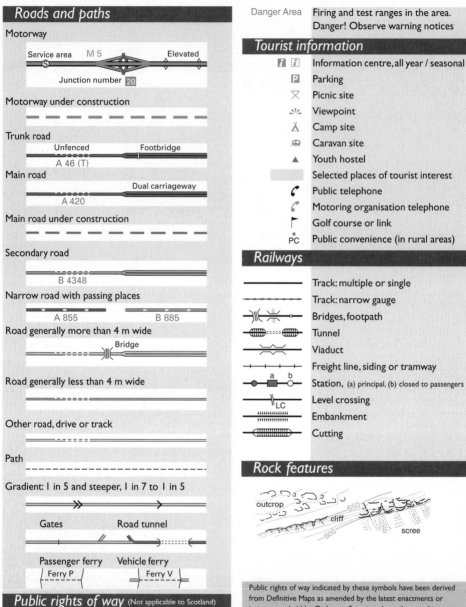

Service area   M 5   Elevated

Junction number 20

Motorway under construction

Trunk road

Unfenced   Footbridge
A 46 (T)

Main road

Dual carriageway
A 420

Main road under construction

Secondary road

B 4348

Narrow road with passing places

A 855   B 885

Road generally more than 4 m wide

Bridge

Road generally less than 4 m wide

Other road, drive or track

Path

Gradient: 1 in 5 and steeper, 1 in 7 to 1 in 5

Gates   Road tunnel

Passenger ferry   Vehicle ferry
Ferry P   Ferry V

Public rights of way (Not applicable to Scotland)

- Footpath
- Bridleway
- Road used as a public footpath
- Byway open to all traffic

Danger Area   Firing and test ranges in the area.
Danger! Observe warning notices

Tourist information

i / i	Information centre, all year / seasonal
P	Parking
✕	Picnic site
☀	Viewpoint
Å	Camp site
⌂	Caravan site
▲	Youth hostel
	Selected places of tourist interest
ℂ	Public telephone
ℂ	Motoring organisation telephone
┌	Golf course or link
PC	Public convenience (in rural areas)

Railways

- Track: multiple or single
- Track: narrow gauge
- Bridges, footpath
- Tunnel
- Viaduct
- Freight line, siding or tramway
- Station, (a) principal, (b) closed to passengers   a   b
- Level crossing   LC
- Embankment
- Cutting

Rock features

outcrop   650   cliff   600   scree

Public rights of way indicated by these symbols have been derived from Definitive Maps as amended by the latest enactments or instruments held by Ordnance Survey and are shown subject to the limitations imposed by the scale of mapping. Further information may be obtained from the appropriate County or London Borough Council

The representation on this map of any other road, track or path is no evidence of the existence of a right of way

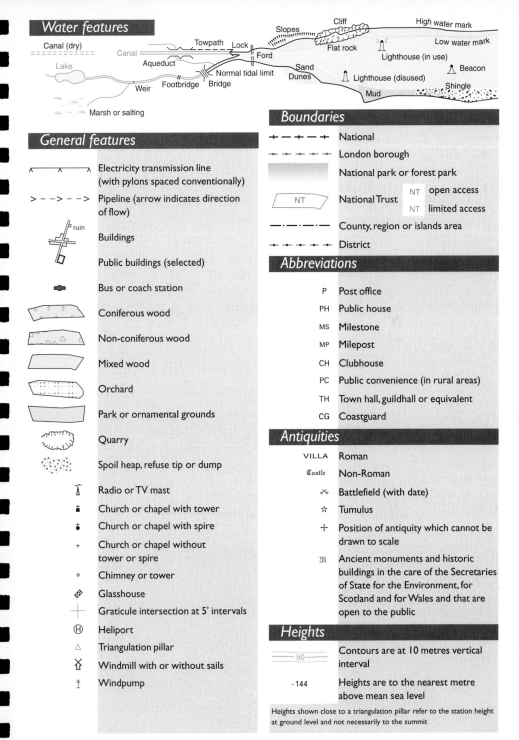

Water features

Canal (dry)
Canal
Lake
Towpath
Lock
Aqueduct
Ford
Weir
Footbridge
Bridge
Normal tidal limit
Marsh or salting

Slopes
Cliff
Flat rock
High water mark
Low water mark
Lighthouse (in use)
Sand
Dunes
Lighthouse (disused)
Mud
Beacon
Shingle

General features

⅄ — ⅄ — ⅄	Electricity transmission line (with pylons spaced conventionally)
> − −> − −>	Pipeline (arrow indicates direction of flow)
⌂ ruin	Buildings
	Public buildings (selected)
⬌	Bus or coach station
	Coniferous wood
	Non-coniferous wood
	Mixed wood
	Orchard
	Park or ornamental grounds
	Quarry
	Spoil heap, refuse tip or dump
ⵣ	Radio or TV mast
♦	Church or chapel with tower
♦	Church or chapel with spire
+	Church or chapel without tower or spire
○	Chimney or tower
⬦	Glasshouse
┼	Graticule intersection at 5' intervals
Ⓗ	Heliport
△	Triangulation pillar
ⵚ	Windmill with or without sails
ⵝ	Windpump

Boundaries

+ — + — +	National
⊶ ⊶ ⊶ ⊶ ⊶	London borough
	National park or forest park
NT	National Trust
— · — · —	County, region or islands area
+ + + + +	District

National Trust: NT open access / NT limited access

Abbreviations

P	Post office
PH	Public house
MS	Milestone
MP	Milepost
CH	Clubhouse
PC	Public convenience (in rural areas)
TH	Town hall, guildhall or equivalent
CG	Coastguard

Antiquities

VILLA	Roman
Castle	Non-Roman
⚔	Battlefield (with date)
☆	Tumulus
+	Position of antiquity which cannot be drawn to scale
ℳ	Ancient monuments and historic buildings in the care of the Secretaries of State for the Environment, for Scotland and for Wales and that are open to the public

Heights

══ 50 ══	Contours are at 10 metres vertical interval
· 144	Heights are to the nearest metre above mean sea level

Heights shown close to a triangulation pillar refer to the station height at ground level and not necessarily to the summit

West from Durham City into the Deerness Valley

This ride offers a number of interesting options. Three of County Durham's railway paths intersect near Broompark at a point which is only 2 km (1¼ miles) from the centre of Durham City. These paths are suitable and recommended for all but racing cycles and, as they follow the valley floor, they avoid a number of hills that the all-tarmac route cannot avoid. Several sections of level, traffic-free cycle path are possible on this ride though there is a perfectly acceptable on-road alternative (with hills). The choice is yours. Valleys always mean hills but this route cleverly misses most of the heavy hills with one exception. The eastern third passes through several ex-mining communities with ordered rows of terraced houses with their neat and tidy gardens. The open road is soon attained and the route zigzags westwards along quiet roads which wend their way across very pleasant undulating countryside.

At Salter's Gate there are fine views of the North Pennines. The return route takes in the Lanchester Valley.

Start

Broompark Picnic Area, off the B6302 southwest of Durham City (GR 252416)

P As above

Distance and grade

54 km (34 miles) – plenty of short cuts but some have hills

🚲🚲🚲 Moderate

🚲🚲🚲🚲 Moderate/ strenuous on-road alternative

Terrain

Generally undulating with one short brute of a hill between Low and High Hedleyhope – not a long walk/push. The on-road option has a steady climb south of Lanchester. There are a number of long downhills. Highest

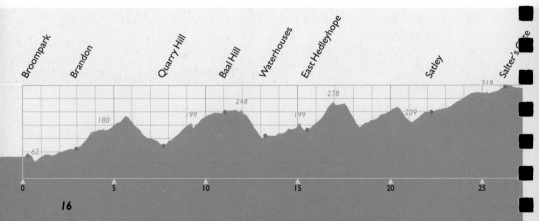

point – Salter's Gate 350 m (1148 ft). Lowest point – near the start 62 m (204 ft)

Nearest railway

Durham City

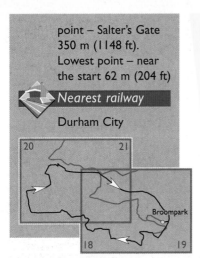

Lanchester 10
Takes its name from a nearby Roman fort built on Dere Street which ran between York and Hadrian's Wall. Now an attractive small town with a village feel to it

Bearpark 11
Close to the Lanchester Valley Walk across the River Browney are the remains of Beaurepaire which was the monks' retreat from the monastery of Durham from which Bearpark takes its name

Langley Park 11
Product of coalmining sometimes used in TV and film dramas. Purpose-built handball wall next to the path beside a row of miner's cottages. This was a popular game in the mining villages of Durham

◀ North Pennines, south of Edmund

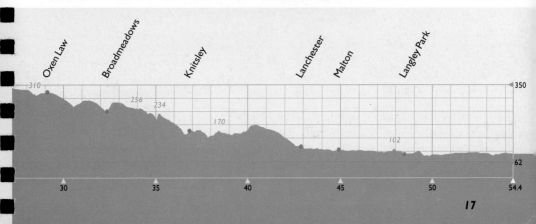

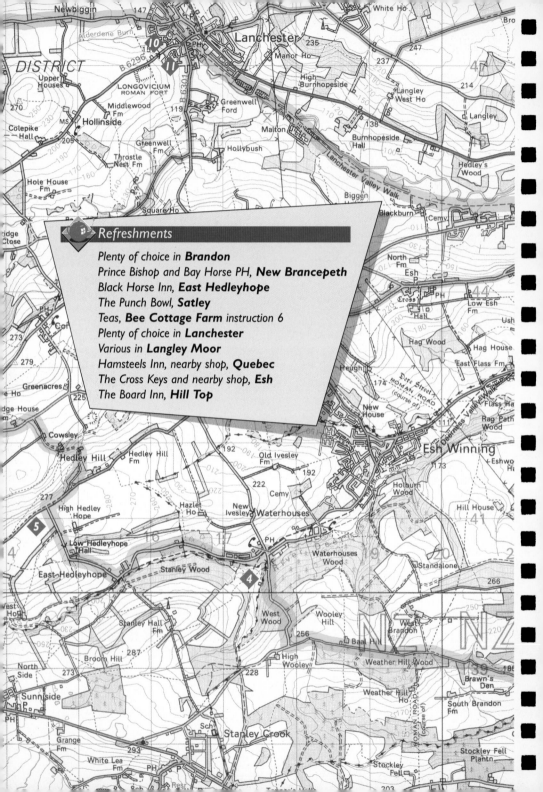

Refreshments

Plenty of choice in **Brandon**
Prince Bishop and Bay Horse PH, **New Brancepeth**
Black Horse Inn, **East Hedleyhope**
The Punch Bowl, **Satley**
Teas, **Bee Cottage Farm** instruction 6
Plenty of choice in **Lanchester**
Various in **Langley Moor**
Hamsteels Inn, nearby shop, **Quebec**
The Cross Keys and nearby shop, **Esh**
The Board Inn, **Hill Top**

1 Join the railway path, turn L. Bear R at path fork 'Brandon, Bishop Auckland'. Cross River Deerness (bridge – short push). Cross 3 roads, then turn R at next T-j to New Brancepeth

2 Turn L 'Pit House 1, New Brancepeth 1½', SA at next T-j. At hill top turn L (downhill)

3 Turn R for 4 km (2½ miles), turn R (NS) downhill to cross ri

4 1st L after crossing Deerness Valley Walk 'East Hedleyhope'. Keep Ivesley Cottages on R. Road bears R to steep hill – what you see is what you get! Levels to B6301

5 Turn R, then L after 400 m (¼ mile) down steep hill to T-j (NS). Turn L to X-roads SA to B6296 (**Or** turn R to Satley PH/phone). Turn L, then 2nd R 'Drover House 1, Salter's Gate 2½'

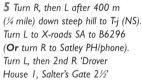

➡ **page 20**

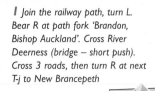

Alternative route

A At Langley Hall Farm turn L, then 1st R to T-j (NS). 1 km steady climb to T-j, turn R (to instruction 2)

Alternative route

See pages 20-21

10 Before Main Street, turn R onto Lanchester Valley Walk at 'P Free' sign (**Or** turn R opposite Blue Bell Inn to T-j for shops & refreshment. Turn R on Station Road, then L after 150 m (165 yd) onto railway path and on-road Route 2)

11 5.5 km (3½ miles) to Langley Park, then the same to 3 paths junction of instruction 1. Turn R to start (**Or** previous L to Durham City)

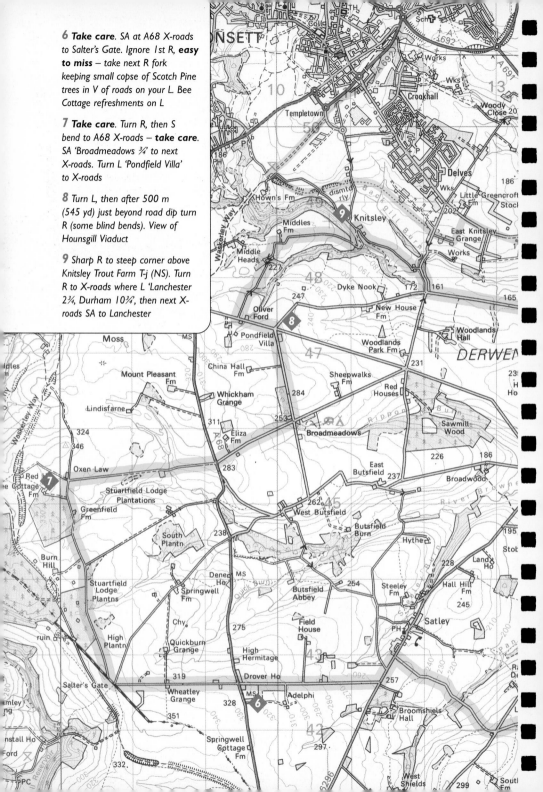

6 *Take care. SA at A68 X-roads to Salter's Gate. Ignore 1st R,* **easy to miss** *– take next R fork keeping small copse of Scotch Pine trees in V of roads on your L. Bee Cottage refreshments on L*

7 *Take care. Turn R, then S bend to A68 X-roads –* **take care**. *SA 'Broadmeadows ¾' to next X-roads. Turn L 'Pondfield Villa' to X-roads*

8 *Turn L, then after 500 m (545 yd) just beyond road dip turn R (some blind bends). View of Hounsgill Viaduct*

9 *Sharp R to steep corner above Knitsley Trout Farm T-j (NS). Turn R to X-roads where L 'Lanchester 2¾, Durham 10¾', then next X-roads SA to Lanchester*

10 *Before Main Street, turn R onto Lanchester Valley Walk at 'P Free' sign (**Or** turn R opposite Blue Bell Inn to T-j for shops & refreshment. Turn R on Station Road, then L after 150 m (165 yd) onto railway path and on-road Route 2)*

11 *5.5 km (3½ miles) to Langley Park, then same to 3 paths junction of instruction 1. Turn R to start (**Or** previous L to Durham City)*

Alternative route

11 *Turn next L after Lanchester Valley Walk (Ford Road) B6301 for 1 km. Turn R for almost 2 km (1½ miles) to T-j 'Greenwell Farm'* **NB** *this is a county road*

B *Turn L, ascend to off-set X-roads. SA to B6301 X-roads. SA to Quebec and on to Esh. SA to Hill Top 'Bearpark 1½, Durham 4' (twice)*

C page 19 *At Board Inn sign bear R; next T-j turn R down to B6302 X-roads. SA up to New Brancepeth T-j*

D page 19 **Either** *turn L, then after 250 m (270 yd) 1st R 'Langley Moor' through Alum Waters to Langley Farm – reverse A to Star, **or** turn L down to railway path, then turn R along it to return to the start*

2 The Consett and Sunderland railway path and Lanchester Valley

An interesting, combination route which utilises an on-road link to connect two excellent railway paths, this circuit can be joined at any point thus avoiding the need to use a vehicle. Commencing at Beamish for descriptive purposes, a clockwise direction is chosen to take advantage of the steep downhill into the Lanchester Valley after first crossing the undulations north and west of Sacriston. The Lanchester Valley railway path is followed through rural County Durham to Lydgetts Lane junction to join Sustrans' Consett and Sunderland railway path and Coast to Coast route. The ex-steelworks town of Consett and its satellite communities is negotiated and a high-level track leads into Annfield Plain. Passing easily through the built up section, the open views and rural atmosphere return as the circuit is completed.

Start

Beamish Country Park (GR 217537)

P As above

Distance and grade

42 km (26 miles) – short route 29 km (18 miles)

Easy

Terrain

Railway paths nearly always follow valleys with, at worst, a gentle gradient; the land between valleys is always higher and this is where the hills are on this ride. The steep hill down into Lanchester needs care. Highest point – Consett 265 m (869 ft). Lowest point – Pelton Fell 70 m (230 ft)

Nearest railway

Chester-le-Street, 3 km (2 miles) east of the route

22

Beamish 1
The biggest open-air museum in Europe featuring all things historical of North East heritage; the Town, Colliery village, Railway Station, Home Farm and Pockerley Manor all with every aspect of a Victorian community in living reality and accessible by tram, bus or on foot

Consett and Sunderland Railway Path
Owned by the the 'paths for people' charity Sustrans (sustainable transport) and developed in conjunction with local Authorities; available for cyclists, walkers, wheelchairs and where appropriate, horse riders. Look out for the spectacular Howns Gill Viaduct, built by Sir Thomas Bouch in 1857, which uses more than 2.5 million bricks. The C2C route shares a section of the railway path and is part of a much larger National Cycle Network. Straddling the North Pennines between the Irish Sea and the North Sea, the 225-km (140-mile) route follows minor roads and traffic-free cycle paths and won the Global Award for Green Tourism in 1996

▼ Drift Mine, Beamish Museum

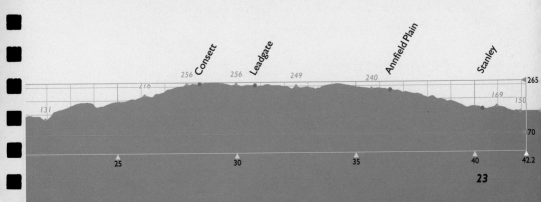

23

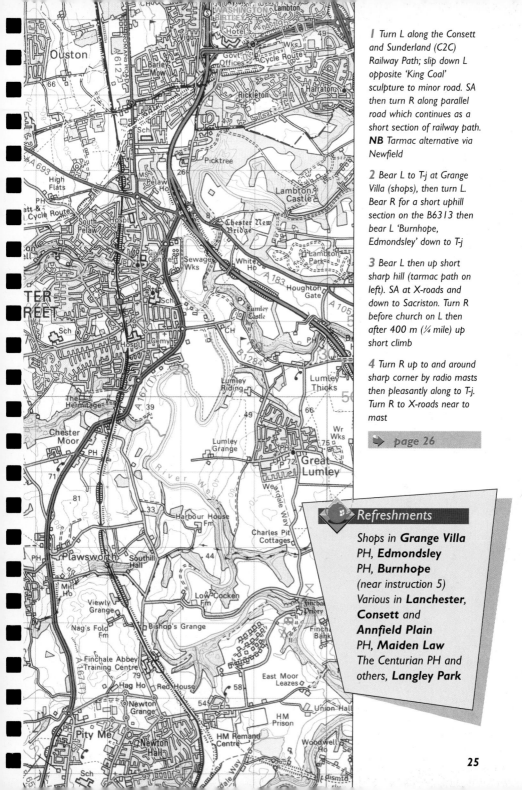

1 Turn L along the Consett and Sunderland (C2C) Railway Path; slip down L opposite 'King Coal' sculpture to minor road. SA then turn R along parallel road which continues as a short section of railway path. **NB** Tarmac alternative via Newfield

2 Bear L to T-j at Grange Villa (shops), then turn L. Bear R for a short uphill section on the B6313 then bear L 'Burnhope, Edmondsley' down to T-j

3 Bear L then up short sharp hill (tarmac path on left). SA at X-roads and down to Sacriston. Turn R before church on L then after 400 m (¼ mile) up short climb

4 Turn R up to and around sharp corner by radio masts then pleasantly along to T-j. Turn R to X-roads near to mast

➡ page 26

Refreshments

Shops in **Grange Villa**
PH, **Edmondsley**
PH, **Burnhope**
(near instruction 5)
Various in **Lanchester**,
Consett and
Annfield Plain
PH, **Maiden Law**
The Centurian PH and
others, **Langley Park**

5 Take care. Turn L, down steeply, to Lanchester. Cross A691 then SA for 200 m (220 yd) to Lanchester Valley Walk

Short cut

SA to Maiden Law X-roads (PH) then again SA and turn R 'Greencroft Industrial Estate' to re-join railway path by small lake on left (see instruction 10)

6 Turn R and follow railway path through attractive countryside to Lydgett's Lane junction (**Or** L for on-road Route 1). Turn L for 400 m (½ mile) to the Howns Gill Viaduct then retrace

7 Turn R from Lanchester (SA from viaduct) and follow C2C directions (either stencils or small blue signs)

8 At Templetown turn L then turn R at

roundabout on marked cycle path. Cross road then after 200 m (220 yd) bear R to cross Delves Lane by Rover Garage (**take care**)

9 SA, then keep sports field on your right to roundabout. Cross by the marked cycle path, then SA to next roundabout (PH). Cross to diagonally opposite point, through the cycle maze and on past 'The Transformers' sculpture to small lake (at instruction 10)

10 SA (see Short cut) opposite lake, then – **easy to miss** – cross A693 by new bridge. Through Annfield Plain, then follow Consett and Sunderland Railway Path to the start

3 Along the Tyne Valley from Haltwhistle

Start

Haltwhistle Railway Station

P As above

Distance and grade

69 km (43 miles)

Easy/moderate

Terrain

Quiet roads and lanes through ever changing scenery; some hills in the western half of the route but otherwise level. Highest point – Crindledykes corner 262 m (860 ft). Lowest point – Tyne Riverside Country Park 1m (3 ft)

Nearest railway

Haltwhistle

This ride is a linear route and follows the line of the picturesque Tyne Valley. From Haltwhistle the usually quiet road to Bardon Mill is taken then, leaving the valley floor behind, the cycle-friendly ascent into Hadrian's Wall country ensues. There is a short, rough section between the main entrance to Vindolanda and the museum at Chesterholm after which the Roman road Stanegate leads eastwards to descend into Newbrough and on through Fourstones. A pleasant, scenic detour provides good views of the River North Tyne to re-join the attractive riverside route into Hexham. There is some height gain beyond Hexham where the route splits to include Corbridge or to take in two castles before descending to the riverside for the remaining part of the ride; first Bywell then Ovingham followed by Low Prudhoe and Wylam until finally Newburn is reached – a most enjoyable expedition.

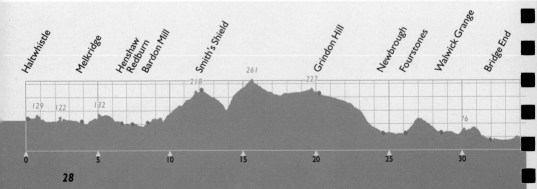

Vindolanda *3*

Extensive site of Roman fort and settlement situated behind Hadrian's Wall with fine museum and re-construction fort. Almost totally self-sufficient in all essentials, the fort was home for the occupying army from AD 80 for several centuries at different levels; it is still under permanent exploration; some 12000 artifacts are found each year and this is projected to continue for the next 150 years

Hexham *7*

Since AD 674 Hexham's history has spanned the centuries: Hexham Abbey has 7th century origins; the Moot Hall was built in about 1400; a tall pillar of red sandstone marks the site of the old market now the centre of the Tuesday market next to the Shambles (long roofed shelter) built in 1766; Tyne Bridge, built in 1793, is the first bridge over the river after the 'Meeting of the Waters' east of Warden

Halton Castle and **Aydon Castle** *9*

Fine 14th-century fortified house chiefly composed of Roman stones; dignified little church largely re-built in 1706 again using Roman stones; interesting dove-cote and pond with resident ducks. Aydon Castle, built in 1300, is also in a fine situation and open to the public

▶ *Hexham Abbey and the memorial cross*

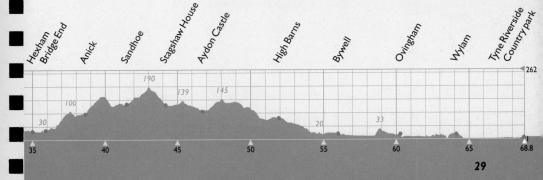

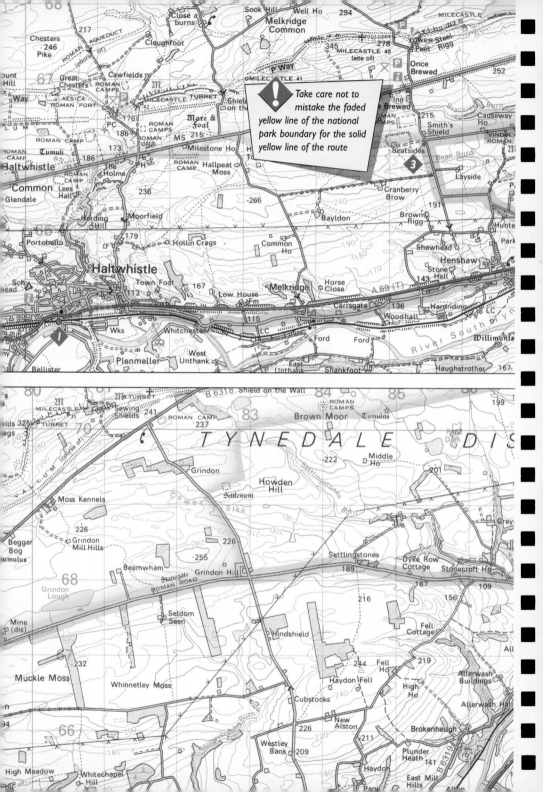

Take care not to mistake the faded yellow line of the national park boundary for the solid yellow line of the route

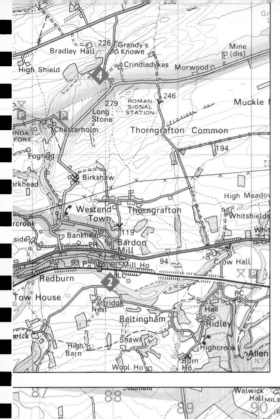

1 *Turn R along old A69 (now down graded) then turn R beyond Esso garage under new bypass (**Or** cross road to cycle along Main Street to the same place)*

2 *Turn L under A69 then keep L to T-j; Turn L then over bridge and turn R; bear R then sharp L and turn R at T-j*

3 *SA to YH, Information Centre and refreshments. Turn R to Vindolanda.* **NB** *short section of rough surface then up steeply to T-j and turn L*

4 *Turn R along Stanegate (Roman road) and enjoy panoramic views before dropping down to Newbrough*

5 *Turn L and climb to Walwick Grange Fm then turn R to Bridge End.* **NB** *The direct route has a dangerous section with blind bends and no verge (improvements planned)*

6 *Cross river then turn L along very pleasant lanes (LC) to Tyne Green*

page 32

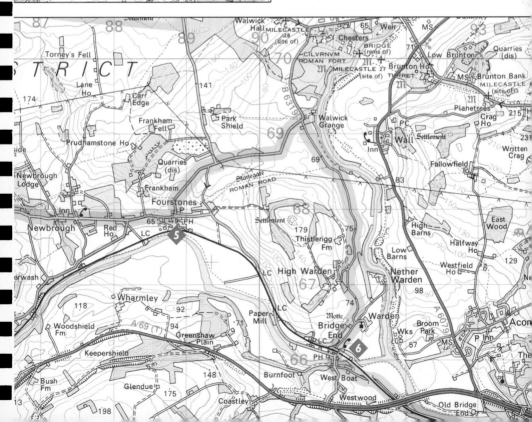

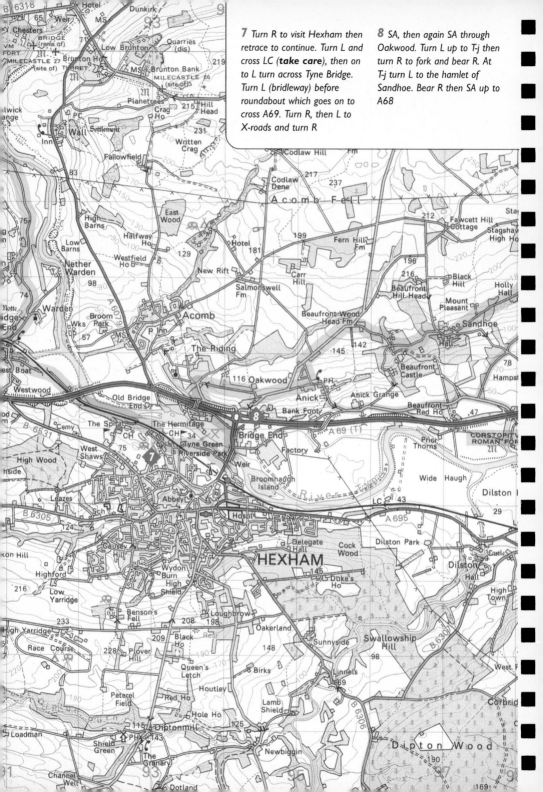

7 Turn R to visit Hexham then retrace to continue. Turn L and cross LC (**take care**), then on to L turn across Tyne Bridge. Turn L (bridleway) before roundabout which goes on to cross A69. Turn R, then L to X-roads and turn R

8 SA, then again SA through Oakwood. Turn L up to T-j then turn R to fork and bear R. At T-j turn L to the hamlet of Sandhoe. Bear R then SA up to A68

9 Take care. Turn R down to next turning L to Halton Castle (**Or** SA, then turn 1st R for a superb descent into Corbridge). Returning from Halton, turn L to Aydon Castle

10 Turn R, then L and then cut back R down to B6530.

Turn L, then turn next R (**take care**) to descend to the banks of the River Tyne

11 SA and bear L at Bywell Bridge (**Or** SA then turn R at next X-roads to visit Bywell)

➡ page 35

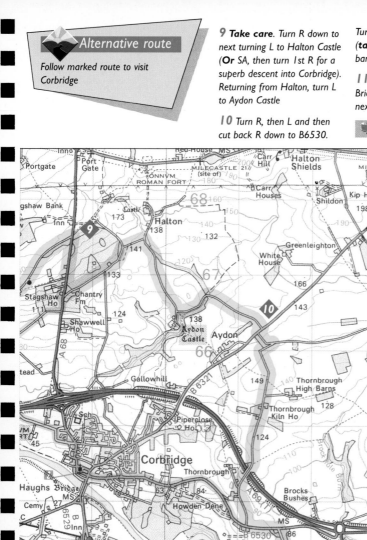

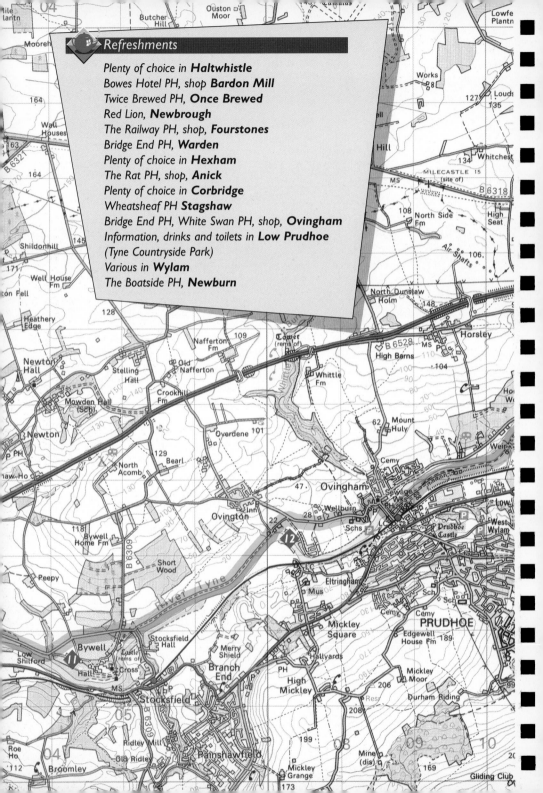

◆ Refreshments

Plenty of choice in **Haltwhistle**
Bowes Hotel PH, shop **Bardon Mill**
Twice Brewed PH, **Once Brewed**
Red Lion, **Newbrough**
The Railway PH, shop, **Fourstones**
Bridge End PH, **Warden**
Plenty of choice in **Hexham**
The Rat PH, shop, **Anick**
Plenty of choice in **Corbridge**
Wheatsheaf PH **Stagshaw**
Bridge End PH, White Swan PH, shop, **Ovingham**
Information, drinks and toilets in **Low Prudhoe**
(Tyne Countryside Park)
Various in **Wylam**
The Boatside PH, **Newburn**

12 Bear R to Ovingham
NB superb packhorse bridge on R. Turn R over metal bridge (**take care**) then turn R into Tyne Riverside Park (toilets). Pass under bridge and follow riverside cycle path past Hagg Fm

13 Turn L before the railway bridge then cross West Wylam Bridge; follow the railway path to the road which leads to the Country Park.

NB The route continues east to Newcastle quayside and on to North Shields (ferry terminals) and Tynemouth. This is a Sustrans Millenium Route and whilst most of the route is in place, some new sections and bridges will not be completed until Easter 2000 but on-road alternatives are possible

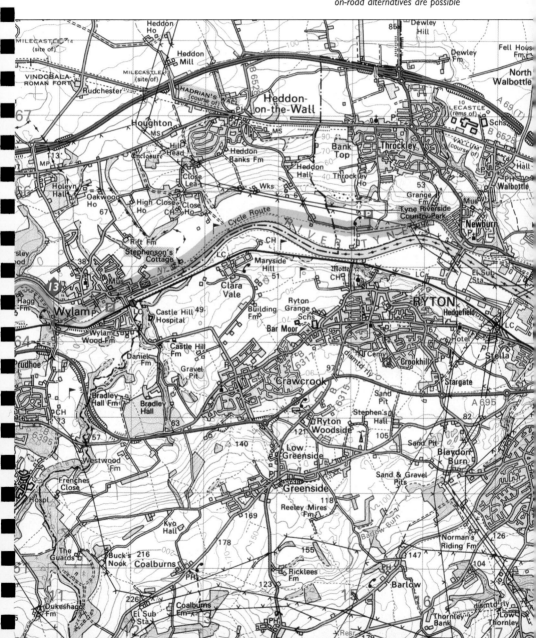

From Stocksfield, to the north and south of the Tyne Valley

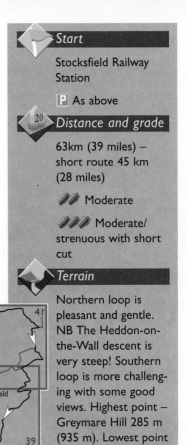

This route offers two excellent rides in one and, in the main, uses quiet lanes and minor roads. The Tyne Valley sections are flat and offer fine cycling through pleasant scenery and can be enjoyed at length (literally) in their own right. Stamfordham is a picturesque village surounded by attractive countryside and also features in on-road Route 6. The Cycle Route past Stephenson's Cottage is recommended for all bikes, as is the onward short-cut route across West Wylam Bridge to Prudhoe. The Southern loop requires more energy but not to any excessive degree so do not be put off if you are reasonably fit. The uphill sections are amply rewarded with matching downhills and the refreshment points are well placed at suitable intervals. In common with almost all of the rides in this book, fine views are included.

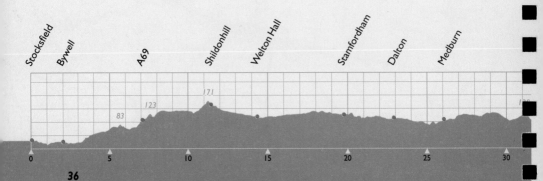

▼ Prudhoe Castle

Places of interest

Bywell 2 (short detour)
Quiet site of historical interest but the original village has long gone; twin churches of St Andrews with its superb Saxon tower known as the White Church (Premontsratensian monks from nearby Blanchland) and St Peters, the Black from the black robed Benedictine monks of Durham. There is an ancient village cross, Bywell Castle (private) and 18th-century Bywell Hall – well worth further investigation

Wylam 10
Cottage birth-place of George Stephenson, the creator of railways, born in 1781; the arched West Wylam Bridge was an earlier construction design on which much larger and more famous bridges were modelled including The Tyne Bridge, The Wear Bridge at Sunderland and even the Sydney Harbour Bridge in Australia

The Lead Road 13/16
Until fairly recent times, lead ore was mined in the North Pennines and smelted at various locations. The lead was then taken by road to main ports or to be turned into pipes etc at Blaydon on Tyne

Refreshments

Shop, **Stocksfield**
Bay Horse Inn, Swinburne Arms, **Stamfordham**
The Swan PH, Three Horse Shoes PH, **Heddon-on-the-Wall**
Tea room and others **Wylam**
Fox and Hounds PH, **Coalburns**
Three horse Shoes PH, **Leadgate**
Dr Syntax, **New Ridley**

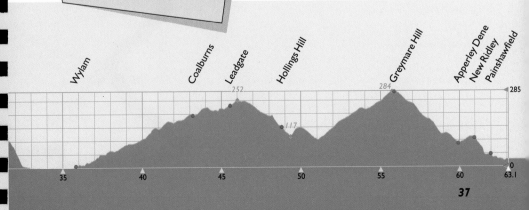

37

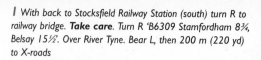

1 With back to Stocksfield Railway Station (south) turn R to railway bridge. **Take care**. Turn R 'B6309 Stamfordham 8¾, Belsay 15½'. Over River Tyne. Bear L, then 200 m (220 yd) to X-roads

2 SA 'Newton 2¼, Styford 2¼, Corbridge 4½'. (**Or** turn L for short detour to Bywell)

➡ **page 40**

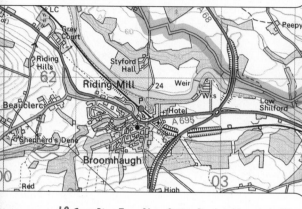

10 Cross River Tyne, SA on Station Road and bear L. At T-j (triangle) bear R 'Sled Road, Bradley Nursery and Gardens'

⬆ Short cut

Stay on railway path to cross West Wylam Bridge to end of railway path and turn R. SA with row of houses on R to Tyne Country Park (toilets), cross metal bridge to T-j in Ovingham, turn L **NB** packhorse bridge on left. Pass school, bear L along river to Bywell. Reverse instruction I to return to the start

11 Turn R then
bear R 'Bradley Hall, Access only' on old road
to gap and traffic lights on left (cattle crossing point). Straight over cattle grid (**take care**)

12 Tarmac ends and lanes fork, bear L (short, un-tarmacked section, suitable for most road bikes, walk if necessary to re-join tarmac). Bear L up to fine views

13 **Easy to miss**. 2nd turn R (NS), with stone stile on left, to T-j (PH). Turn R (steady climb) bear R 'Hedley-on-the-Hill' past PH to X-roads (has track on R – see off-road Route 3)

14 Turn L down to T-j and turn L to B6309. Bear L 'Ebchester 1, Durham 16 (A691)' then after 200 m (220 yd) bear R 'Shotleyfield 2¾, Carterway Heads 4'

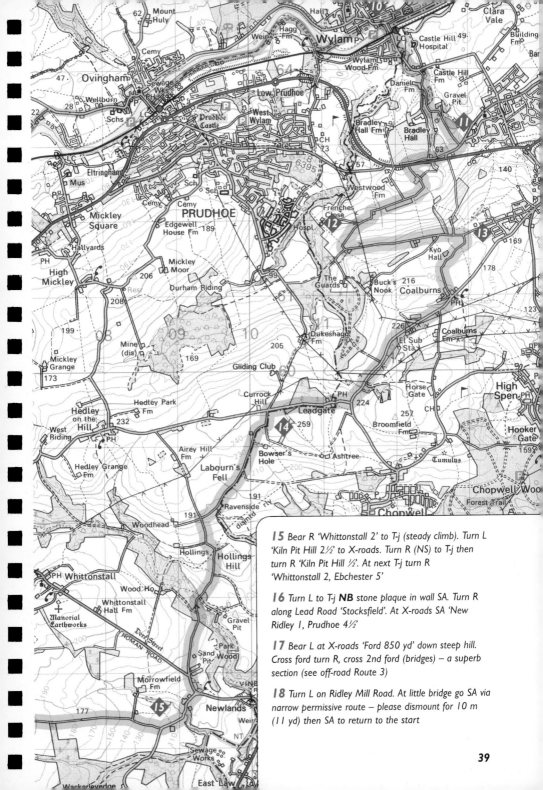

15 Bear R 'Whittonstall 2' to T-j (steady climb). Turn L 'Kiln Pit Hill 2½' to X-roads. Turn R (NS) to T-j then turn R 'Kiln Pit Hill ½'. At next T-j turn R 'Whittonstall 2, Ebchester 5'

16 Turn L to T-j **NB** stone plaque in wall SA. Turn R along Lead Road 'Stocksfield'. At X-roads SA 'New Ridley 1, Prudhoe 4½'

17 Bear L at X-roads 'Ford 850 yd' down steep hill. Cross ford turn R, cross 2nd ford (bridges) – a superb section (see off-road Route 3)

18 Turn L on Ridley Mill Road. At little bridge go SA via narrow permissive route – please dismount for 10 m (11 yd) then SA to return to the start

3 Turn L – **take care** – then after 400 m (¼ mile) turn R 'Thornbrough ½, Aydon 2' to fork, bear R (NS)

4 Bear R 'Welton 2, Stelling 2¼'. X-roads SA 'Welton 1, Stelling 5'

5 SA 'Stamfordham 4'. SA at X-roads 'Stamfordham 3, Belsay 9'. Zigzag to Stamfordham!

6 SA 'Ponteland 6, Newcastle 13¾' (**Or** Turn L into village and link to on-road Route 6 at instructions 3/4)

7 SA 'Dalton 1¼, Ponteland 5¼' over bridge bear R. T-j turn R 'Newburn 6, Wylam 8, Newcastle 10'

8 Turn R 'Stamfordham 5, Matfen 8½'. **Easy to miss**. 250 m (270 yd) **after** next farm on R turn L 'Single Track Road, Unsuitable for HGVs'. Turn R (in effect SA)

9 For Wylam via railway path turn L before petrol station, then next R 'Heddon ¼'. **NB** Hadrian's Wall on L. Turn L just after bus shelter (NS) 'Station Road leading to Heddon Haughs' after 25 m (27 yd). PH 100 m (110 yd) beyond bus shelter. Long stretch downhill through farm to railway path, turn R to Wylam (toilets)

Alternative route

Wylam by road. SA passing petrol station, then turn L 'Close House ½' to Wylam. Turn L 'Crawcrook 1½, Station ¼, RVI Castle Hill ¾' (PH, shops, toilets)

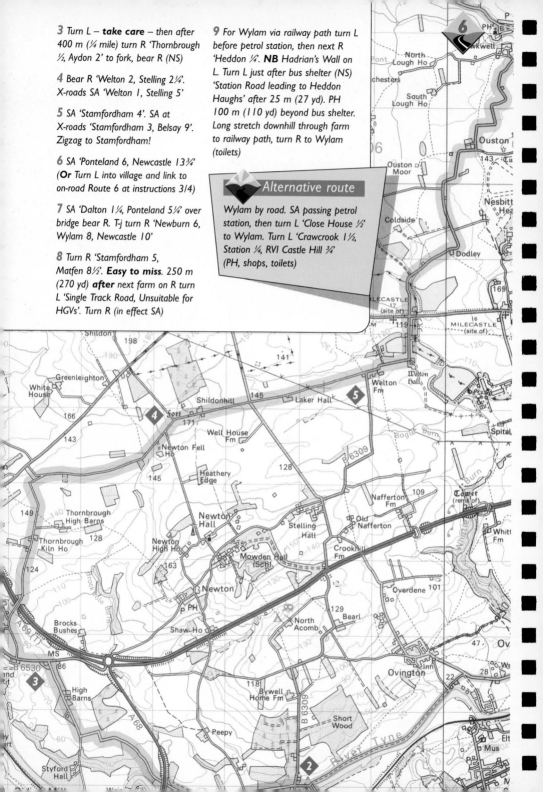

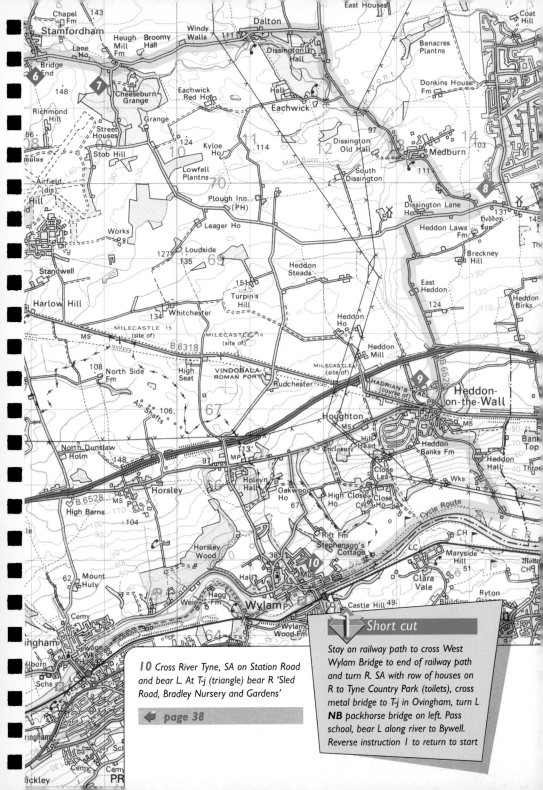

10 Cross River Tyne, SA on Station Road and bear L. At T-j (triangle) bear R 'Sled Road, Bradley Nursery and Gardens'

◀ page 38

Short cut

Stay on railway path to cross West Wylam Bridge to end of railway path and turn R. SA with row of houses on R to Tyne Country Park (toilets), cross metal bridge to T-j in Ovingham, turn L **NB** packhorse bridge on left. Pass school, bear L along river to Bywell. Reverse instruction 1 to return to start

5 The north Tyne Valley, east of Bellingham and west of Wark

Start

Village green, Wark

P 1 km north of Wark on east side of river, opposite Gold Island

20 Distance and grade

62 km (39 miles) – short route 45 km (28 miles)

///// Moderate/strenuous

Terrain

Largely undulating, this hilly ride has marvellous views and can be ridden in either direction. Highest point – Green Rigg 291 m (955 ft). Lowest point – Wark 78 m (257 ft)

Nearest railway

Hexham, 13 km (8 miles) south of instruction 2

As with any route, grading is always prone to subjectivity and that is without attempting to take into account the many variables such as weather, bike condition and fitness. This tour is graded Moderate/strenuous because if it is windy it will tend to lean toward the category of Strenuous due to its position. This is a fine ride and would merit inclusion in any guide book so pick your day and go for it. Following the River North Tyne to Gunnerton the ride then climbs gently and pleasantly northwards to offer magnificent views of the surrounding fells and distant Kielder Forest. The long, narrow downhill past Sweethope Lough leads on to East and West Woodburn before the scenic but steady climb which preceeds the steep descent into Bellingham. The route climbs out of the valley and on over rolling pasture land to circumnavigate the edge of Wark Forest whilst offering a superb array of ever-changing vistas before threading its way back to Wark.

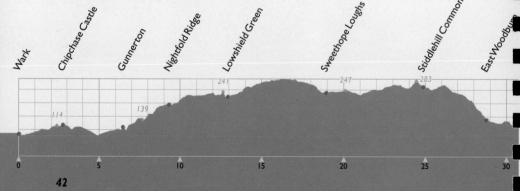

▼ *Hareshaw Linn, near Bellingham*

Chipchase Castle 1

Splendid-looking combination of mid-14th-century tower with a Jacobean mansion and Georgian additions and alterations; also mid-18th-century chapel. The house and grounds are only open to the public in June but the gardens and nursery are open more frequently

Bellingham 9

Pronounced 'Bellinjum'; a small, pleasant old market town quietly slumbering on the banks of the River North Tyne and bordering the fells and moors of the Borderlands. The area abounds in interesting legends which are well worth researching (The Charlton Spur, The Long Pack and the Healing Spring)

43

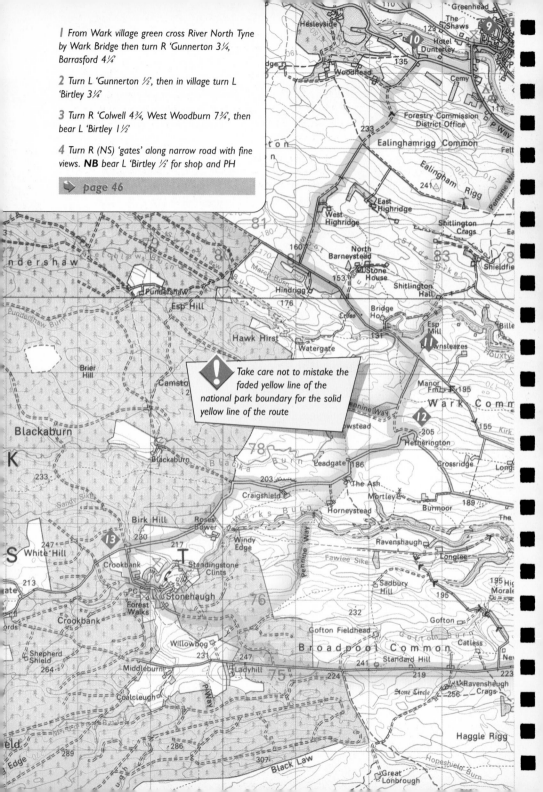

1 *From Wark village green cross River North Tyne by Wark Bridge then turn R 'Gunnerton 3¼, Barrasford 4¼'*

2 *Turn L 'Gunnerton ½', then in village turn L 'Birtley 3¼'*

3 *Turn R 'Colwell 4¾, West Woodburn 7¾', then bear L 'Birtley 1½'*

4 *Turn R (NS) 'gates' along narrow road with fine views.* **NB** *bear L 'Birtley ½' for shop and PH*

⮕ **page 46**

Take care not to mistake the faded yellow line of the national park boundary for the solid yellow line of the route

5 Turn R (NS) to A68 X-roads. SA on narrow road, pass Sweethope Loughs (lakes), then turn L on wider road 'West Woodburn 5'

6 Turn R for 350 m (380 yd) on A68 then turn R 'East Woodburn 1¼, Monkridge 4¼ – please **take care** and use the wide verge if necessary; do not wait in middle of road for R turn

7 Turn L (NS) to A68 then turn R – use footpath on R to access PH and shop and avoid crossing A68 twice

8 Turn L opposite PH 'Bellingham 4¼'

9 Turn L at Main Street then pass clock tower on your L and cross river. Turn R (NS) 'Unsuitable for HGVs' and Northumberland National Park sign (curlew)

Short cut

Turn L down to Bellingham and rejoin route at instruction 9

← page 45

! Take care not to mistake the faded yellow line of the national park boundary for the solid yellow line of the route

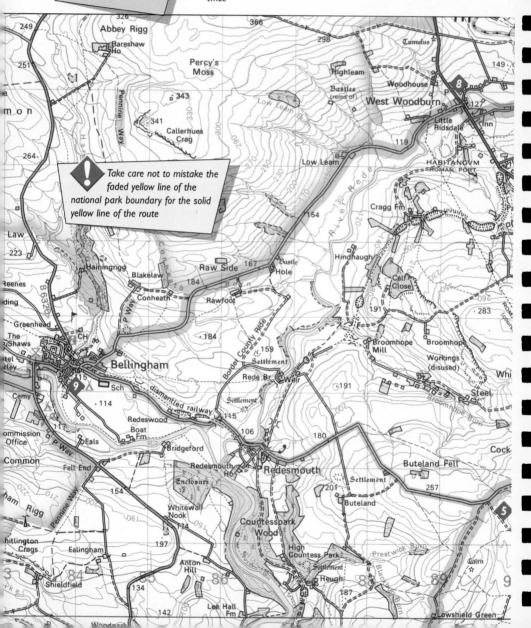

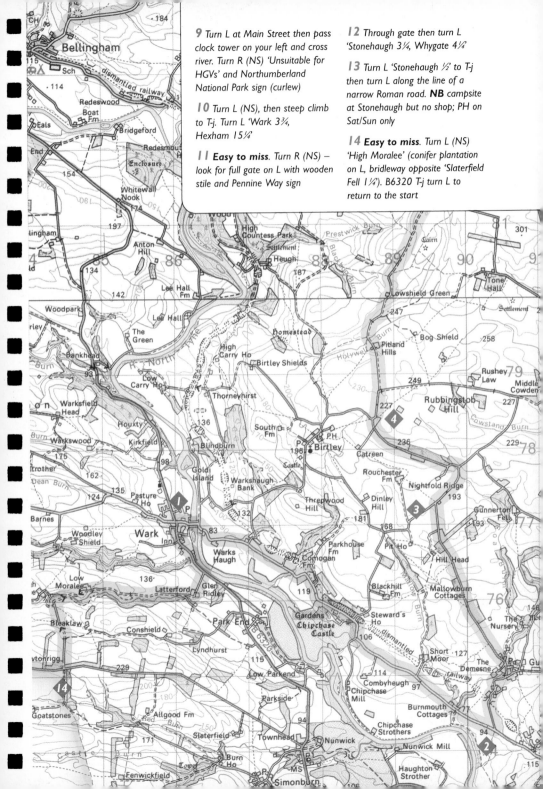

9 Turn L at Main Street then pass clock tower on your left and cross river. Turn R (NS) 'Unsuitable for HGVs' and Northumberland National Park sign (curlew)

10 Turn L (NS), then steep climb to T-j. Turn L 'Wark 3¾, Hexham 15¼'

11 *Easy to miss*. Turn R (NS) – look for full gate on L with wooden stile and Pennine Way sign

12 Through gate then turn L 'Stonehaugh 3¼, Whygate 4¼'

13 Turn L 'Stonehaugh ½' to T-j then turn L along the line of a narrow Roman road. **NB** campsite at Stonehaugh but no shop; PH on Sat/Sun only

14 *Easy to miss*. Turn L (NS) 'High Moralee' (conifer plantation on L, bridleway opposite 'Slaterfield Fell 1¼'). B6320 T-j turn L to return to the start

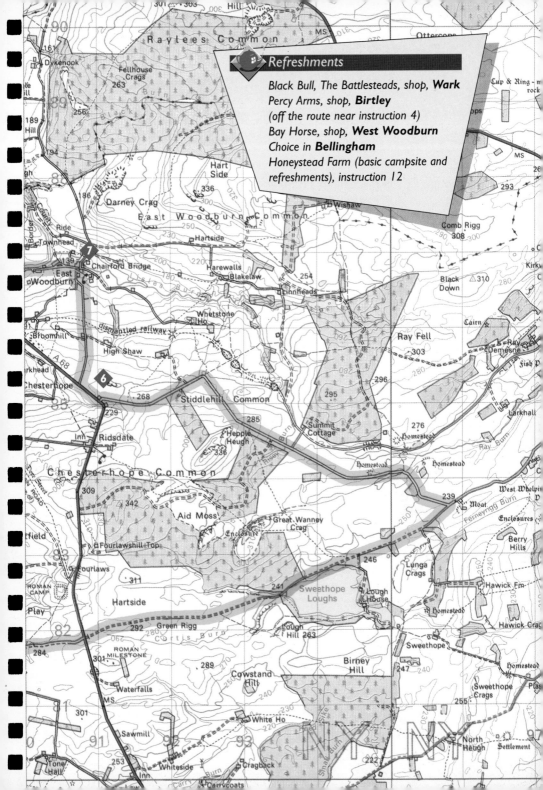

Refreshments

Black Bull, The Battlesteads, shop, **Wark**
Percy Arms, shop, **Birtley**
(off the route near instruction 4)
Bay Horse, shop, **West Woodburn**
Choice in **Bellingham**
Honeystead Farm (basic campsite and
refreshments), instruction 12

6 Northwest of Ponteland, along quiet roads to Capheaton

Although this ride starts at Ponteland, Newcastle is not a great distance away. There is a choice of railway path or road through Darras Hall luxury estate to reach the Medburn road where the ride really begins. On to bonny Stamfordham with its spacious village green and old gaol house and then to the lovely village of Matfen. Northwards to Capheaton noted for its attractive stone cottages – all of which give this ride a timeless feel. On-road Route 7 is crossed at Makemerich which is a farm not a promise! Narrow lanes run gently downhill through unspoilt countryside to end this truly enjoyable tour.

Start
Main Street or Darras Hall, Ponteland

P Parking behind Station Cottages, Ponteland

Distance and grade
56 km (35 miles)

Easy/moderate

Terrain
Very gently but almost imperceptibly rising to the top of the loop and returning with the aid of gravity. Highest point – Ingoe Moor 230 m (755 ft). Lowest point – Ponteland 57 m (188 ft)

Nearest railway

Metro Station at Newcastle airport (folding bikes only)

Refreshments

Plenty of choice in **Ponteland**
Tea rooms, **Capheaton**
Black Bull, shop, **Matfen**
Bay Horse, Swinburne Arms, shop, **Stamfordham**
Plough Inn at instruction 2

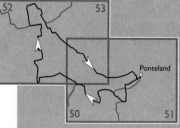

52   53

Ponteland

50   51

Ponteland | Medburn | Eachwick | Stamfordham | Fenwick | Matfen | Ingoe 229

132   121   130   129   130   146

0   5   10   15   20   25

Belsay Hall, Castle and Gardens *(close to the route)* 10
Castle is 14th century, the Grecian style Hall is 19th century, 12 ha (30 acres) of landscaped gardens with a unique rock garden. Altogether a most remarkable country estate and well worth a visit

Capheaton Hall 9
Fine stone country house built in 1688 by Robert Trollope (also Netherwitton Hall) with matching estate cottages

Other Halls
Dissington Hall (unseen); Eachwick Hall (good view); Cheeseburn Grange near Stamfordham; Matfen Hall – a Cheshire Home recently converted into a golf club

▼ *Matfen Cross and houses*

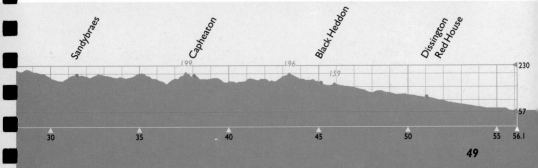

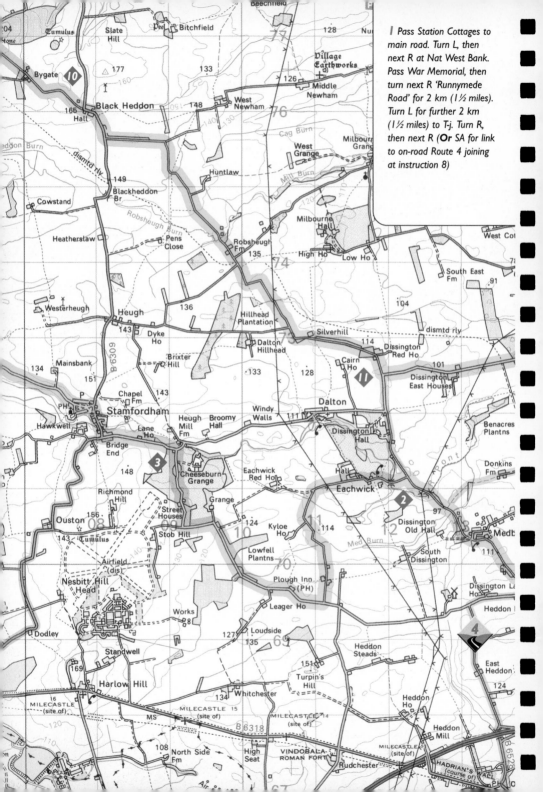

Pass Station Cottages to main road. Turn L, then next R at Nat West Bank. Pass War Memorial, then turn next R 'Runnymede Road' for 2 km (1½ miles). Turn L for further 2 km (1½ miles) to T-j. Turn R, then next R (**Or** SA for link to on-road Route 4 joining at instruction 8)

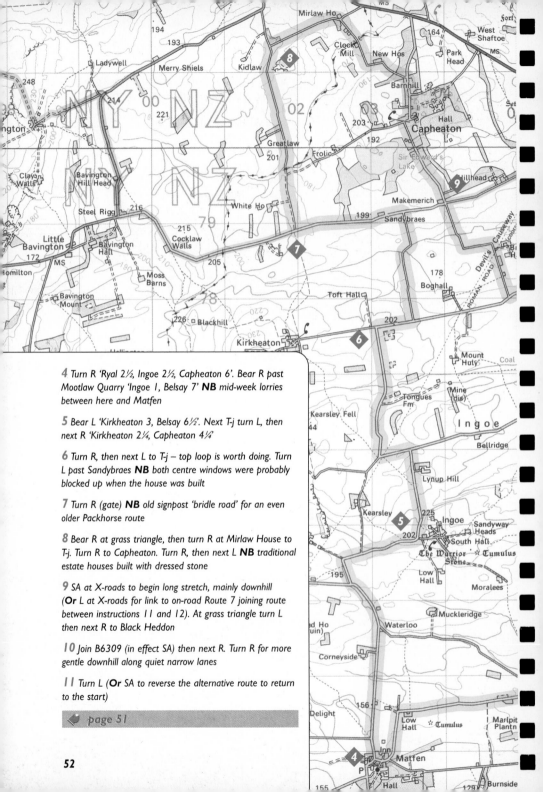

4 Turn R 'Ryal 2½, Ingoe 2½, Capheaton 6'. Bear R past Mootlaw Quarry 'Ingoe 1, Belsay 7' **NB** mid-week lorries between here and Matfen

5 Bear L 'Kirkheaton 3, Belsay 6½'. Next T-j turn L, then next R 'Kirkheaton 2¼, Capheaton 4¼'

6 Turn R, then next L to T-j – top loop is worth doing. Turn L past Sandybraes **NB** both centre windows were probably blocked up when the house was built

7 Turn R (gate) **NB** old signpost 'bridle road' for an even older Packhorse route

8 Bear R at grass triangle, then turn R at Mirlaw House to T-j. Turn R to Capheaton. Turn R, then next L **NB** traditional estate houses built with dressed stone

9 SA at X-roads to begin long stretch, mainly downhill (**Or** L at X-roads for link to on-road Route 7 joining route between instructions 11 and 12). At grass triangle turn L then next R to Black Heddon

10 Join B6309 (in effect SA) then next R. Turn R for more gentle downhill along quiet narrow lanes

11 Turn L (**Or** SA to reverse the alternative route to return to the start)

📖 page 51

 Alternative route

For Cycle Path through Darras Hall turn R at Nat West Bank, then turn L into park to bridge. Bear R then follow interesting cycle path. **Easy to miss**. At church cross road and cut behind shops then sharp R. At end of road **either** turn L to join main route, on to T-j, turn R then next R, **or**, for robust bikes, turn R then next L along bridleway to road above Medburn, then turn R

2 Turn L 'Eachwick ½, Wylam 5' to T-j then turn R 'Stamfordham 5, Matfen 8½'

3 Turn L 'Stamfordham 1, Matfen 4½' then turn R into Stamfordham. Bear L at large grass triangle **NB** old gaol on the right

page 52

10 Join B6309 (in effect SA) then next R. Turn R for more gentle downhill along quiet narrow lanes

11 Turn L (**Or** SA to reverse the alternatvie route to return to the start)

12 Turn R (busy road – but there is a footpath as far as the bend). Turn R after bend down Fox Covert Lane then next L to reverse instruction 1 back to the start

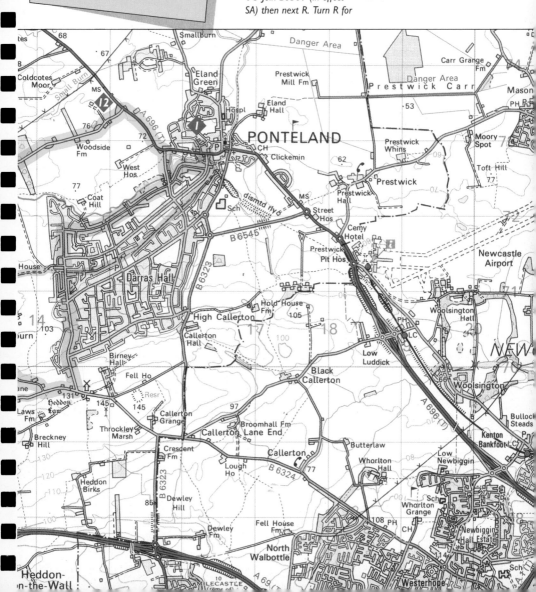

Westward to Wallington from Morpeth of Mitford

The countryside which lies to the west of Morpeth is nothing short of a rural treasure trove in terms of cottages and mansions, rivers and ravines; woods and farmsteads; lakes, castles and crags. The scenery is as varied as the ride itself – changing character dramatically as the route unfolds. At first, the roads are wide and full of purpose but gradually they change to reveal hidden gems by the side of the picturesque ribbons along which you ride. Whilst numerous large houses are visible in this area, Wallington Hall is the centre-piece and this stately home can be easily seen from the road as you cycle past. The busy A696 is crossed twice at right angles and the route passes close to the Great and Little Wanney. These are two north-facing crags extruding from the windswept fells which this route ventures across using unbelievably quiet and narrow byways. Bolam Lake Country Park is visited on the return leg but this journey of discovery saves the best till last.

Start

River Wansbeck Country Park on B6343, Morpeth (GR 189862)

P As above

Distance and grade

67 km (42 miles)

Moderate

Terrain

Generally undulating but without any significant hills. Highest point – Great Bavington 246 m (807 ft). Lowest point – Morpeth 26m (86 ft)

Nearest railway

Morpeth

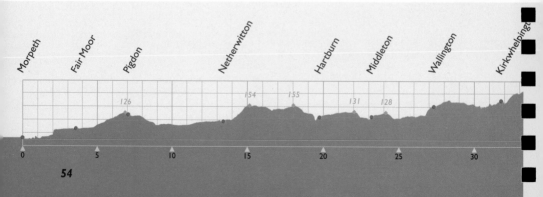

54

Plenty of choice in **Morpeth**
Plough Inn, **Mitford**
The Ox Inn, **Middleton**
The Stable Coffee Shop, **Bolam West Houses**
(near instruction 14)
Dyke Neuk 🍴🍴,
off the route north of **Meldon**

Places of interest

Morpeth 1

An ancient and attractive town that lies on a peninsular of the River Wansbeck. Morpeth is said to be the most beautiful town in the county. Numerous interesting buildings and architectural styles; Museum of Northumbrian bagpipes

Wallington Hall 6

Built by Sir William Blackett near the middle of 18th century, later owned by the Trevelyan family who eventually gave it and its large estate to become one of the first National Trust properties. Has French Chateau style and is full of artistic interest – a very worthwhile visit

▼ *The Clock Tower, Wallington Hall*

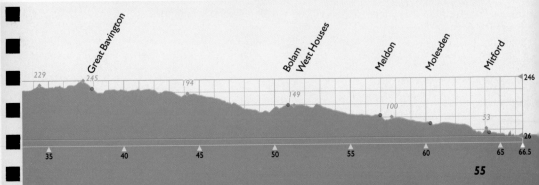

1 West along the B6343 to Mitford. Turn R before bridge **NB** old sign 'St Leonard's Road, Benridge, Pigdon', up short, steep hill to T-j

2 Turn L 'Netherwitton 6½, Pigdon 2½, Stanton 4¾'. Keep R at bend, turn L 'Pigdon 1, Netherwitton 4'. L then R near Stanton

3 Over bridge then turn L 'Longwitton, Cambo'. Follow Z bend, then turn L 'Meldon 4, Morpeth 8'

4 Turn R 'Hartburn 1¾, Scot's Gap 5'. Turn R (NS) at T-j on B6343 to Hartburn cross

➜ *page 58*

15 Turn L 'Whalton 4, Bolam ¾' **NB** Bolam Hall has reverse 'ha ha' (sunken field behind wall on L, to retain stock without wall being visible)

16 Bear L (NS) over old railway bridge, then bear L 'Meldon Village'. Turn R 'Molesden 1¾' bear R at 'No Entry'. **NB** Pill box on L – this road was defended in World War 2! Bear L at West Coldside 'No Entry' to Mitford

17 At T-j turn R, then next R after weir. Turn L after 600 m (650 yd) to town centre

4 *Turn R 'Hartburn 1¾, Scot's Gap 5'. Turn R (NS) at T-j on B6343 to Hartburn cross*

5 *Bear L 'Angerton 1, Middleton 2' SA 'Middleton 1¾'* **NB** *old bridge in field past PH. Turn L at T-j 'Bolam 3½, Belsay 5, Cambo 2½'*

6 *At T-j turn R. At ornate bridge T-j turn R to pass Wallington Hall*

7 *At X-roads turn L 'Kirkwhelpington'. Turn L at public telephone 'toilets', then bear R to A696*

8 **Take care**. *SA 'Carrycoates 6, Great Bavington 4, Plashetts 2½'*

9 *Turn L 'Great Bavington 1'* **NB** *Whinsill Fault, columnar dolerite rock's re-appearance between Roman Wall and Craster*

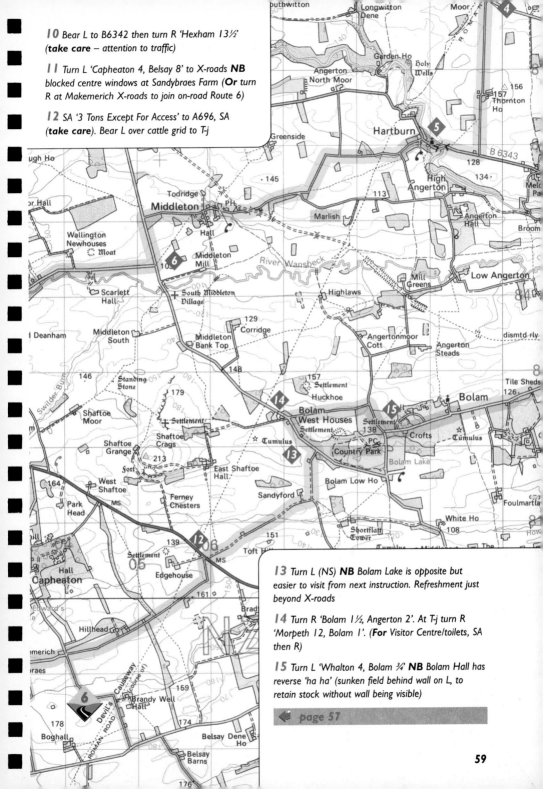

10 Bear L to B6342 then turn R 'Hexham 13½' (**take care** – attention to traffic)

11 Turn L 'Capheaton 4, Belsay 8' to X-roads **NB** blocked centre windows at Sandybraes Farm (**Or** turn R at Makemerich X-roads to join on-road Route 6)

12 SA '3 Tons Except For Access' to A696, SA (**take care**). Bear L over cattle grid to T-j

13 Turn L (NS) **NB** Bolam Lake is opposite but easier to visit from next instruction. Refreshment just beyond X-roads

14 Turn R 'Bolam 1½, Angerton 2'. At T-j turn R 'Morpeth 12, Bolam 1'. (**For** Visitor Centre/toilets, SA then R)

15 Turn L 'Whalton 4, Bolam ¾' **NB** Bolam Hall has reverse 'ha ha' (sunken field behind wall on L, to retain stock without wall being visible)

◀ page 57

Northeast of Morpeth to Cresswell on the coast

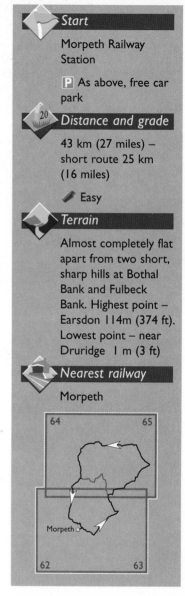

Morpeth is an ideal starting point for a number of rides in this book and for several rides which are not included in this volume. This is a short ride as it fits into the neat rectangle which has the A1 and the A1068 on the vertical sides and the A197 and B6345 on the horizontals. It is, nevertheless, a circular ride and crosses two of the main roads in relative safety to include the first of a series of visits to the magnificent Northumbrian coastline. Out of Morpeth, via pretty Bothal, the urban fringe is gradually left behind as you progress easily and pleasantly towards the coast. The route heads northwards with dunes on your right hand and the taste of the salt air on your lips before cutting inland past Widdrington. Quiet country roads lead on through Tritlington and Hebron until you emerge on the outskirts of Morpeth. There are two large opencast workings which are located in the centre of this ride but be assured, they are well screened and should not spoil your enjoyment.

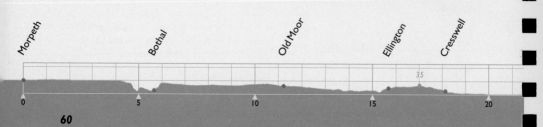

▶ *The River Wansbeck and St George's Church, Morpeth*

Places of interest

Bothal 2

Picturesque hamlet close to the wooded River Wansbeck; substantial stone cottages guarded over by the remains of the ancient 13th-century castle built by Robert Bartram as a smaller scale Dunstanburgh Castle. View of tall, stately gatehouse and nearby is the fine 13th-century church with 14th-century alterations and additions

Cresswell and Widdrington 6/7

Old fishing village with 14th-century Cresswell tower house or peel tower where unspoilt sandy beaches turn to rugged cliffs. Fresh-water Nature Reserve at Druridge Links; Chibburn Presbytery, a 14th-century house of the Knights of St John of Jerusalem recently restored. Druridge Bay has nature reserves and several kilometres of dunes and wide sandy beaches. Widdrington was the location of a little-known French landing in 1692

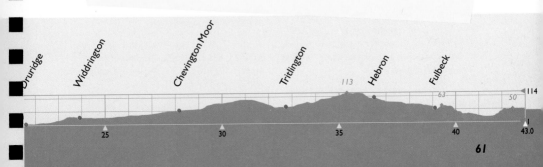

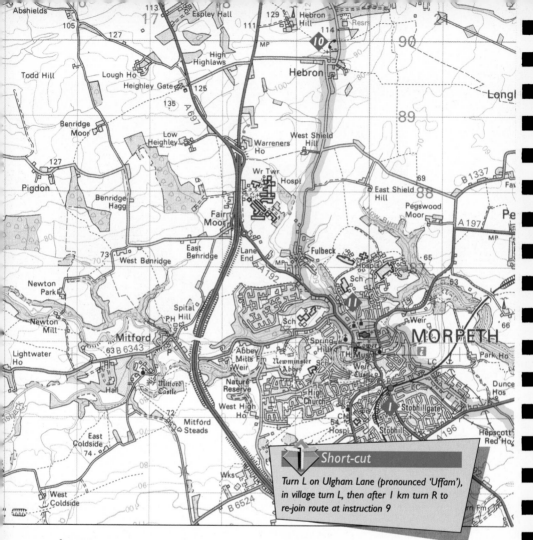

Short-cut

Turn L on Ulgham Lane (pronounced 'Uffam'), in village turn L, then after 1 km turn R to re-join route at instruction 9

1 *Set off with the main line on your L over LC (sidings). After railway footbridge turn R through small industrial estate to A196. Turn L over bridge (path) then turn R (NS). At T-j turn L (NS)*

2 *Turn R then L (almost SA) 'Bothal 1¼, Pegswood 1½' to A1068*

3 *Cross over to path opposite then keep R of A197 for 150 m (165 yd) to cyclists crossing point (islands). Turn L back along cycle path (north side of A197) to T-j, then turn R 'Longhirst'*

4 *Keep R to T-j beyond LC. SA to A1068 and turn L, on to obvious T-j at instruction 5*

5 *Turn L 'Linton ½', then after 200 m (220 yd) bear R along rail path to cross A1068 to T-j*

page 64

10 *Turn L 'Morpeth, Longhirst, Pegswood' then, after just over 1 km, bear R (in effect SA) at grass triangle. At A192 turn L to traffic lights*

11 *Turn L 'Manchester Street', then turn R, then L to A197 T-j. Turn R to mini roundabout, then turn L keeping 'Old Red Bull PH' on your L. **Easy to miss** turn R, then L by Ambulance Station to cross River Wansbeck (bridge). Up to LC (mainline) to return to start*

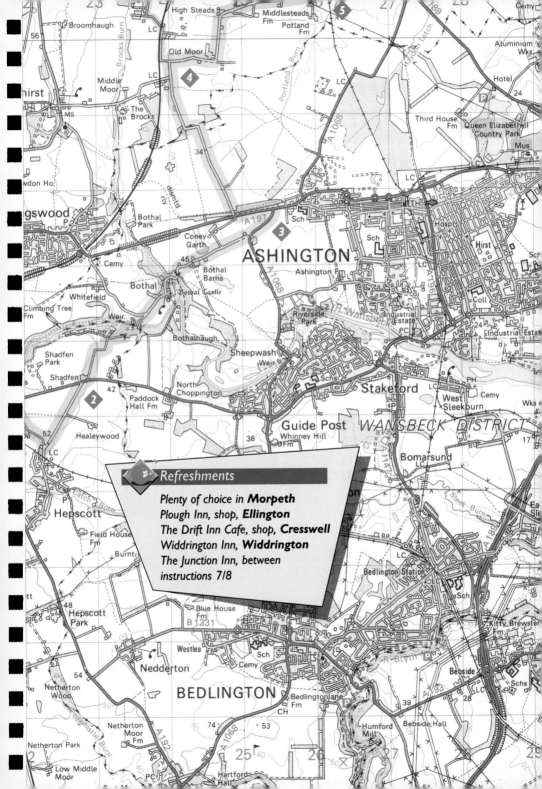

Refreshments

Plenty of choice in **Morpeth**
Plough Inn, shop, **Ellington**
The Drift Inn Cafe, shop, **Cresswell**
Widdrington Inn, **Widdrington**
The Junction Inn, between
instructions 7/8

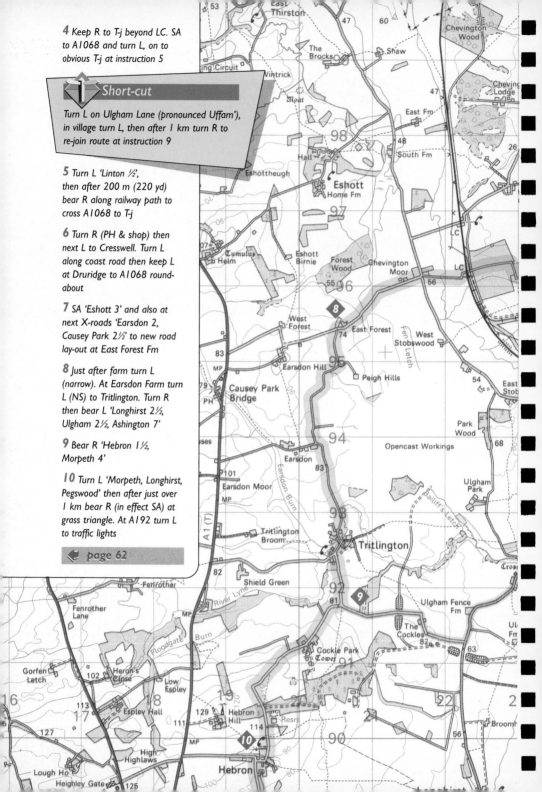

4 Keep R to T-j beyond LC. SA to A1068 and turn L, on to obvious T-j at instruction 5

Short-cut

Turn L on Ulgham Lane (pronounced Uffam'), in village turn L, then after 1 km turn R to re-join route at instruction 9

5 Turn L 'Linton ½', then after 200 m (220 yd) bear R along railway path to cross A1068 to T-j

6 Turn R (PH & shop) then next L to Cresswell. Turn L along coast road then keep L at Druridge to A1068 roundabout

7 SA 'Eshott 3' and also at next X-roads 'Earsdon 2, Causey Park 2½' to new road lay-out at East Forest Fm

8 Just after farm turn L (narrow). At Earsdon Farm turn L (NS) to Tritlington. Turn R then bear L 'Longhirst 2½, Ulgham 2½, Ashington 7'

9 Bear R 'Hebron 1½, Morpeth 4'

10 Turn L 'Morpeth, Longhirst, Pegswood' then after just over 1 km bear R (in effect SA) at grass triangle. At A192 turn L to traffic lights

◀ page 62

Northwest of Morpeth to Rothbury, returning via The Fords

9

Start

River Wansbeck Country Park on B6343, Morpeth (GR 189862)

P As above

Distance and grade

73 km (43 miles) – short route 52 km (31 miles)

Moderate/ strenuous

Terrain

Predominantly quiet rural roads; a wonderful circuit with many options – can be done either way. The three fords are located at the bottom of short sharp descents/ascents and all need care. Highest point – Simonsides 247 m (810 ft). Lowest point – Morpeth 26 m (86 ft)

Nearest railway

Morpeth

Northumberland is full of gems and Rothbury is one of them. Being in a valley, hills are inevitable but this tour uses the contours to the best advantage hence the ride's figure-of-eight shape. The final loop takes the line of least resistance to first of all drop into the utterly charming Coquet Valley and then to climb back out again for the return journey. There is an optional loop at the start of the tour and numerous short-cut possibilities in between. The full circuit to Rothbury via the descent to Great Tosson is recommended for the exceptional views of the Cheviot Hills and the surrounding countryside which this section of the route affords. The cycling prior to this point and throughout the return route is no less enjoyable and the three fords are as picturesque as they are unexpected.

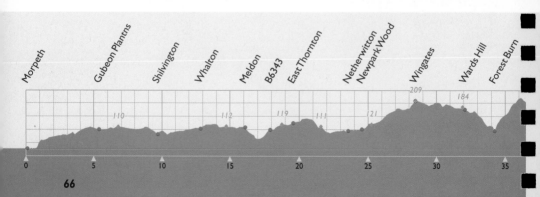

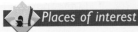
Meldon 3 *and* Netherwitton 5

Disused Morpeth/Rothbury railway line which remains almost fully intact but in multi ownership. A small and humble 13th-century church with tomb of Sir William Fenwick in full armour – the bridge over the Wansbeck is said to be haunted by his wife 'Meg o Meldon'. Attractive double-arched bridge (near instruction 5) beyond which lies the 17th-century Netherwitton Hall built by Anthony Trollope; Newpark Wood is noted for the King and Queen oaks

Rothbury 9

The capital of Coquetdale surrounded by fascinating history and misty legends; Lordenshaw is a large, prehistoric camp containing many 'cup and ring' marked rocks whose meaning is not understood. Newton Park is part of the great deer park enclosed by Robert Rogerson in 1275; the road follows an ancient packhorse route to Great Tosson with its 10 m (33 ft) high peel tower

▲ *Coquet Valley, near Rothbury*

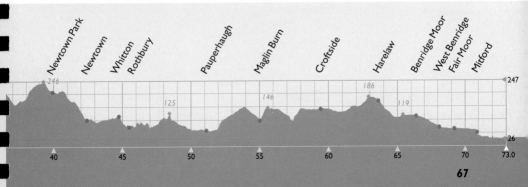

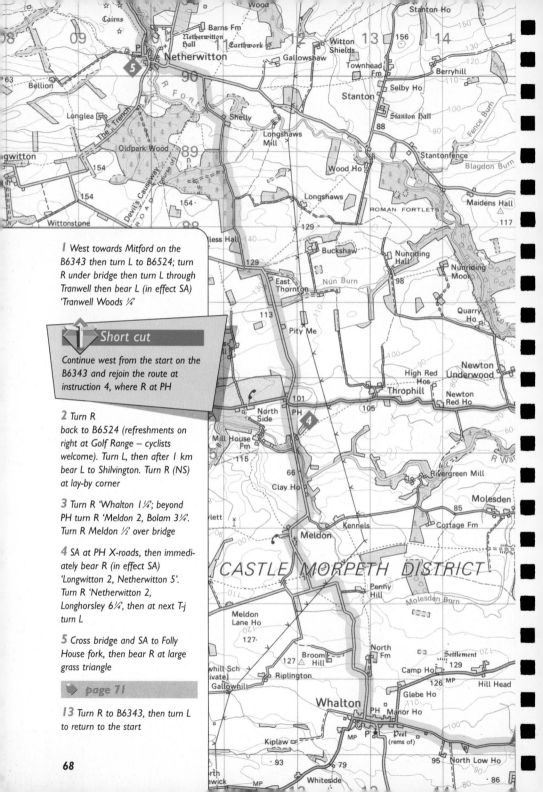

1 West towards Mitford on the
B6343 then turn L to B6524; turn
R under bridge then turn L through
Tranwell then bear L (in effect SA)
'Tranwell Woods ¼'

⬆ Short cut

Continue west from the start on the
B6343 and rejoin the route at
instruction 4, where R at PH

2 Turn R
back to B6524 (refreshments on
right at Golf Range – cyclists
welcome). Turn L, then after 1 km
bear L to Shilvington. Turn R (NS)
at lay-by corner

3 Turn R 'Whalton 1¼'; beyond
PH turn R 'Meldon 2, Bolam 3¼'.
Turn R Meldon ½' over bridge

4 SA at PH X-roads, then immedi-
ately bear R (in effect SA)
'Longwitton 2, Netherwitton 5'.
Turn R 'Netherwitton 2,
Longhorsley 6¼', then at next T-j
turn L

5 Cross bridge and SA to Folly
House fork, then bear R at large
grass triangle

13 Turn R to B6343, then turn L
to return to the start

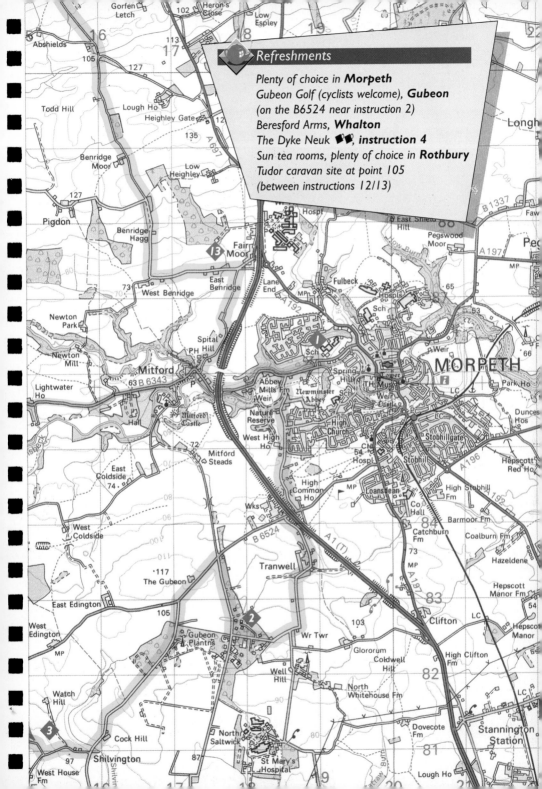

Refreshments

Plenty of choice in **Morpeth**
Gubeon Golf (cyclists welcome), **Gubeon**
(on the B6524 near instruction 2)
Beresford Arms, **Whalton**
The Dyke Neuk, *instruction 4*
Sun tea rooms, plenty of choice in **Rothbury**
Tudor caravan site at point 105
(between instructions 12/13)

Take care not to mistake the faded yellow line of the national park boundary for the solid yellow line of the route

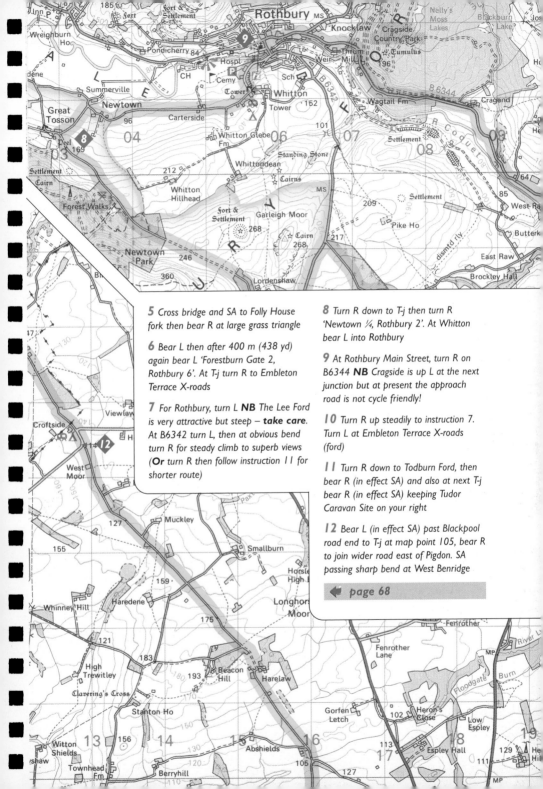

5 Cross bridge and SA to Folly House fork then bear R at large grass triangle

6 Bear L then after 400 m (438 yd) again bear L 'Forestburn Gate 2, Rothbury 6'. At T-j turn R to Embleton Terrace X-roads

7 For Rothbury, turn L **NB** The Lee Ford is very attractive but steep – **take care**. At B6342 turn L, then at obvious bend turn R for steady climb to superb views (**Or** turn R then follow instruction 11 for shorter route)

8 Turn R down to T-j then turn R 'Newtown ¼, Rothbury 2'. At Whitton bear L into Rothbury

9 At Rothbury Main Street, turn R on B6344 **NB** Cragside is up L at the next junction but at present the approach road is not cycle friendly!

10 Turn R up steadily to instruction 7. Turn L at Embleton Terrace X-roads (ford)

11 Turn R down to Todburn Ford, then bear R (in effect SA) and also at next T-j bear R (in effect SA) keeping Tudor Caravan Site on your right

12 Bear L (in effect SA) past Blackpool road end to T-j at map point 105, bear R to join wider road east of Pigdon. SA passing sharp bend at West Benridge

⬅ *page 68*

A coastal circuit from Alnwick via Warkworth and Alnmouth

*T*his ride takes in some of the highlights of Northumberland's coast and threads them together by means of quiet roads and country lanes. Warkworth and Alnmouth are as attractive as they are different; Craster has a special charm of its own and there is not one metre of the entire length of coastline connecting all three places which is less than magnificent. South and up from Alnwick to Shilbottle through pleasant countryside before curving back north to the picture-postcard large village/small town of Warkworth which is dominated by its castle. The route turns inland and gently climbs back towards Shilbottle before descending into the old seaside port of Alnmouth with its tidal harbour and now tiny fishing fleet. On past traditional Northumbrian fishing cobles to Boulmer then once more inland via Longhoughton and Howick Hall to return to the sea again at Craster before minor roads lead back to Alnwick – the Northumberland coast at its best.

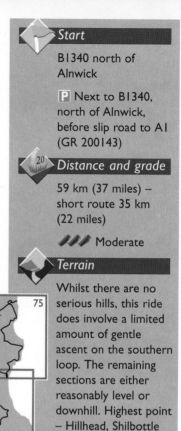

Start

B1340 north of Alnwick

P Next to B1340, north of Alnwick, before slip road to A1 (GR 200143)

Distance and grade

59 km (37 miles) – short route 35 km (22 miles)

/// Moderate

Terrain

Whilst there are no serious hills, this ride does involve a limited amount of gentle ascent on the southern loop. The remaining sections are either reasonably level or downhill. Highest point – Hillhead, Shilbottle 172 m (564 ft). Lowest points – sea level

Nearest railway

Alnmouth, on the route

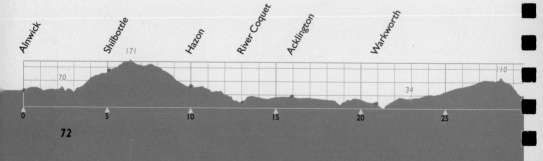

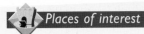

Warkworth 6
The town of the proud castle and the lowly hermitage set above the wooded banks of the River Coquet; a place where legends and myths merge with historical fact! The 14th-century hermitage and chapel, carved out of rock further upstream, is reputedly the finest in the country

Alnmouth 8
Built in 1150 and grew to become a significant North East sea port; on the hill to the south stands the cross of St Cuthbert but the nearby Norman church of St Waleric was finally blown away on Christmas Day 1806 when a storm changed the course of the River Aln and cut off the site from the town. Warkworth/Alnmouth dunes and expansive beaches are clean, open and sandy

Craster 11
Picturesque fishing village with a tiny harbour built in 1906 by the Craster family in memory of a brother who died on active service in Tibet; now famous for Craster kippers (smoked herring). Dunstanburgh Castle stands in isolated splendour along the cliffs to the north. Cullernose Point, complete with guillimot colony teetering and swooping on white-washed basalt ledges, is well worth stopping for

▶ *The River Coquet and Warkworth Castle*

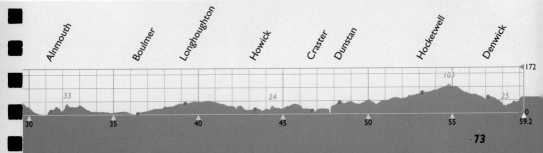

1 Up B1340 to Alnwick and turn L at the monument, then next R 'Swimming Pool, Sports Centre'. Residential road to Alnwick RFC; at roundabout turn L down Willowburn Ave to pass under A1 then turn R 'Shilbottle 2½'

➡ **page 76**

8 SA to Foxbury fork and turn R 'Boulmer, Longhoughton'. Sharp turn L to Longhoughton

9 Turn R 'North End' and keep R at obvious bend (point 49) then Bear R (in effect SA) 'Howick 1¼, Craster 3'

10 Turn L 'Howick' (red reflectors on fence) then at T-j turn L 'Craster 2' to X-roads

11 Turn R to Craster/Dunstanburgh Castle, then retrace to X-roads via Dunstan. After PH bear L 'Alnwick 6¾'. Turn R 'Alnwick 6½' and SA at next cross-roads 'Alnwick 4½' to Hocketwell

12 Turn L 'Longhoughton 2¼, Howick 4, Lesbury 4'

13 Turn R 'Denwick 1½, Alnwick 4' (**NB** Lime kilns in field on right and magnificent beech trees). At T-j turn R (NS) and at B1340 bear L to return to the start or into Alnwick

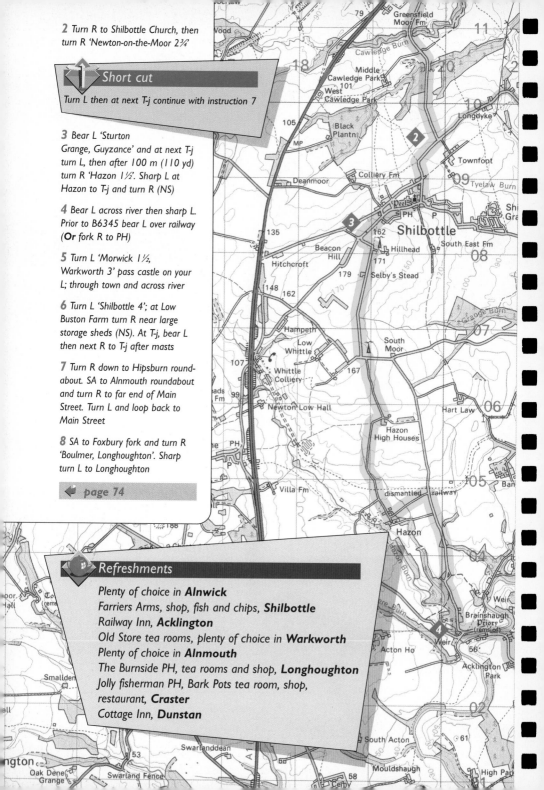

2 Turn R to Shilbottle Church, then turn R 'Newton-on-the-Moor 2¾'

1 **Short cut**

Turn L then at next T-j continue with instruction 7

3 Bear L 'Sturton Grange, Guyzance' and at next T-j turn L, then after 100 m (110 yd) turn R 'Hazon 1½'. Sharp L at Hazon to T-j and turn R (NS)

4 Bear L across river then sharp L. Prior to B6345 bear L over railway (**Or** fork R to PH)

5 Turn L 'Morwick 1½, Warkworth 3' pass castle on your L; through town and across river

6 Turn L 'Shilbottle 4'; at Low Buston Farm turn R near large storage sheds (NS). At T-j, bear L then next R to T-j after masts

7 Turn R down to Hipsburn round-about. SA to Alnmouth roundabout and turn R to far end of Main Street. Turn L and loop back to Main Street

8 SA to Foxbury fork and turn R 'Boulmer, Longhoughton'. Sharp turn L to Longhoughton

◀ page 74

Refreshments

Plenty of choice in **Alnwick**
Farriers Arms, shop, fish and chips, **Shilbottle**
Railway Inn, **Acklington**
Old Store tea rooms, plenty of choice in **Warkworth**
Plenty of choice in **Alnmouth**
The Burnside PH, tea rooms and shop, **Longhoughton**
Jolly fisherman PH, Bark Pots tea room, shop, restaurant, **Craster**
Cottage Inn, **Dunstan**

West of Alnwick, through the Vale of Whittingham

Alnwick lies on a cross-roads of long, straight highways which, although they exist for historical reasons, do not generally aid the route planner. Nevertheless, as a base for cycle touring, Alnwick has much to commend it and the hills which shelter the county town on its western flank are not a serious proposition given some ingenuity and a decent breakfast. The climb out of Alnwick does not go on forever and is soon forgotten as the views of the route ahead beckon and entice. The rewarding descent through Bolton and on into the Vale of Whittingham is a portent of the quiet lanes and magnificent countryside that lie ahead. After a stop in picturesque Whittingham, continue on past Callaly with its magnificent tall beeches and wend your way pleasantly on to just north of Powburn. The route follows yet more rural roads to the attractive village of Eglingham and two short detours minimise the use of the relatively quiet road back into Alnwick.

Start

Prudhoe Road, Alnwick

P Next to B1340, north of Alnwick, before slip road to A1 (GR 200143)

Distance and grade

67 km (42 miles) – short route 46 km (29 miles)

Moderate

Terrain

Many kilometres of easy cycling interspersed with several hills – the downhills more than compensate. Highest point – Yetlington 200 m (656 ft). Lowest point – Alnwick 29 m (96 ft)

Nearest railway

Alnmouth, 7 km (4 miles) east of the route

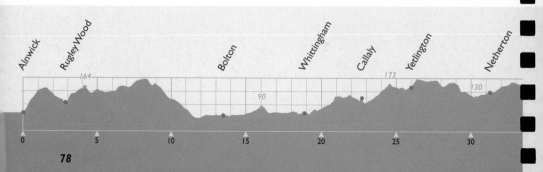

Alnwick 1
Rich in heritage, steeped in history and over-flowing in character, the walled town of Alnwick, pronounced 'Annick', with its imposing gateways, is the county town of Northumberland. It is the domain of the House of Percy and the magnificent castle dominates the town and its past

The Vale of Whittingham 4
Charming village astride the narrow River Aln and was once an important staging post on the Newcastle to Edinburgh road set in the midst of a wide, flat valley. The Whittingham Sword, pronounced 'Whittingjum', was discovered in c.1850 and pre-dates 550 BC

Eglingham 8
Pronounced 'Eglingjum', a pretty little village with an interesting past; a nearby ancient earthwork called the Ringses, Eglingham Hall built on the site of an old peel tower where Cromwell once spent the night then quarrelled next morning with his host Henry Ogle. The exceptionally long church was built on a site granted to the monastery of Lindisfarne in 738 by King Coelwulf

▶ The River Aln and Alnwick Castle

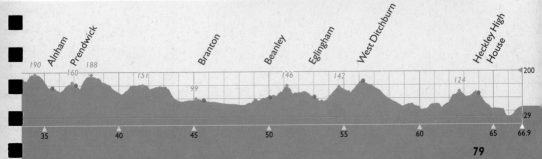

1 With the bus station down R, turn L up B6341. After 700 m (765 yd) turn L keeping Golf Course on your L, then on to T-j turn R to X-roads; turn R to B6341

2 Turn R for 300 m (328 yd) (path) then L. Turn next R over ford (bridge) to X-roads

3 Turn L, then SA at Bolton to next L and on to A697 X-roads

4 *Take care* – SA, at next T-j turn L into Whittingham. Turn 2nd R to T-j at Callaly

➥ page 83

10 SA to fork (grass triangle) bear L 'Eglingham 2¾'. **NB** Stone dovecote on the left

11 At T-j turn R, then bear L after 700 m (765 yd) to 'West Ditchburn 1¾'. Turn sharp R to rejoin B6346

12 Turn R for 5 km (3 miles), then SA to T-j above Heckley High House Farm. Turn R back to B6346

13 Turn L to return to Alnwick and the start

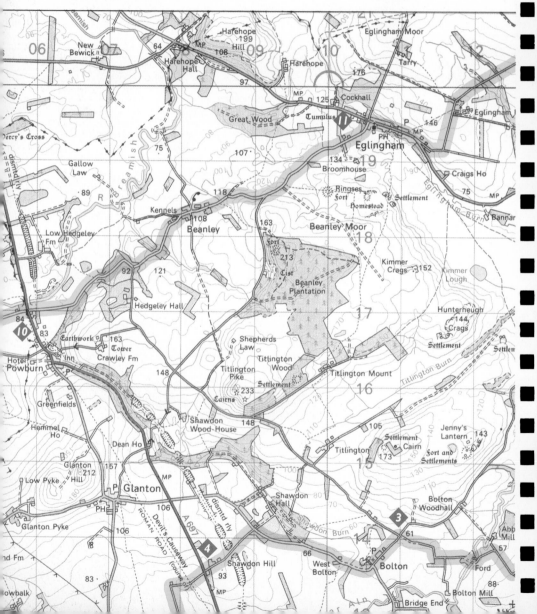

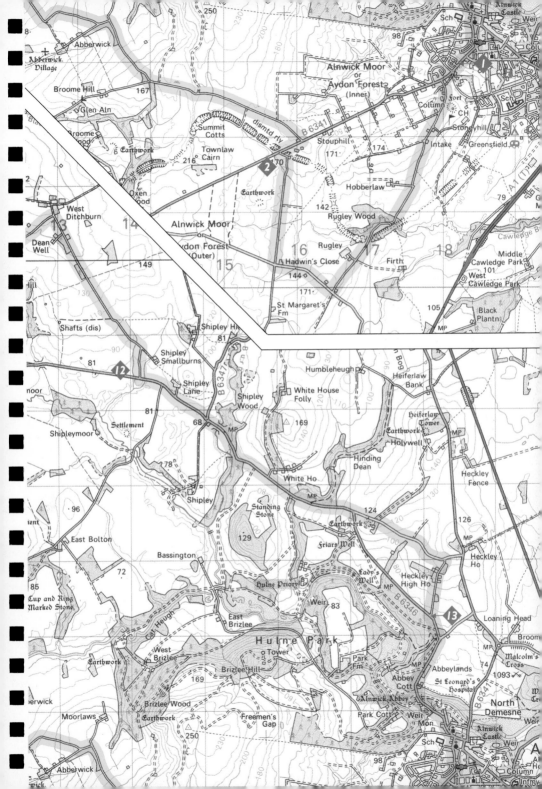

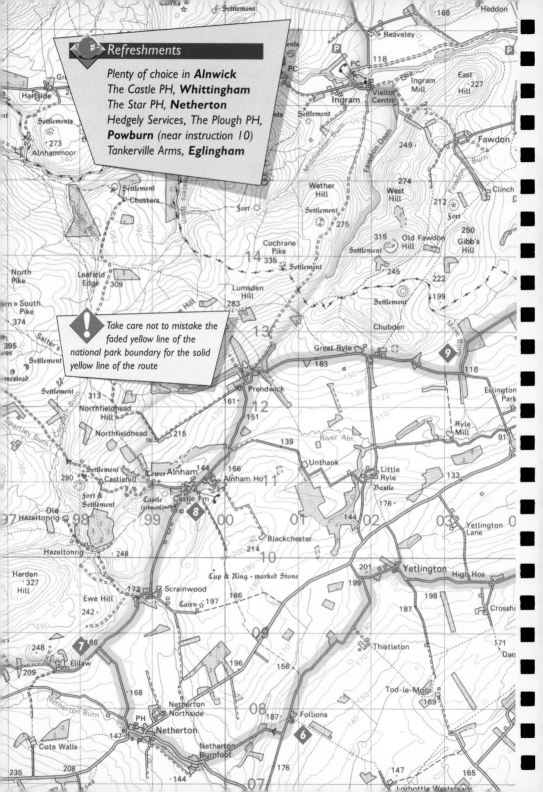

Refreshments

Plenty of choice in **Alnwick**
The Castle PH, **Whittingham**
The Star PH, **Netherton**
Hedgely Services, The Plough PH,
Powburn (near instruction 10)
Tankerville Arms, **Eglingham**

Take care not to mistake the
faded yellow line of the
national park boundary for the solid
yellow line of the route

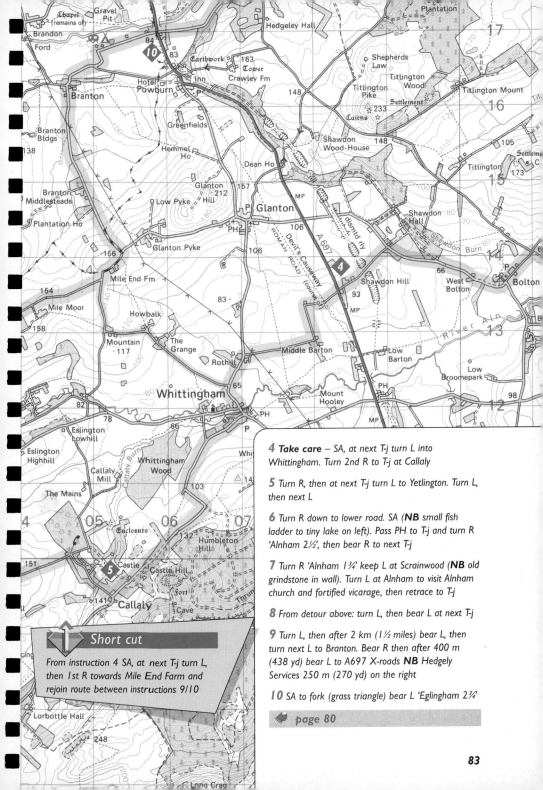

Short cut

From instruction 4 SA, at next T-j turn L, then 1st R towards Mile End Farm and rejoin route between instructions 9/10

4 *Take care* – SA, at next T-j turn L into Whittingham. Turn 2nd R to T-j at Callaly

5 Turn R, then at next T-j turn L to Yetlington. Turn L, then next L

6 Turn R down to lower road. SA (**NB** small fish ladder to tiny lake on left). Pass PH to T-j and turn R 'Alnham 2½', then bear R to next T-j

7 Turn R 'Alnham 1¾' keep L at Scrainwood (**NB** old grindstone in wall). Turn L at Alnham to visit Alnham church and fortified vicarage, then retrace to T-j

8 From detour above: turn L, then bear L at next T-j

9 Turn L, then after 2 km (1½ miles) bear L, then turn next L to Branton. Bear R then after 400 m (438 yd) bear L to A697 X-roads **NB** Hedgely Services 250 m (270 yd) on the right

10 SA to fork (grass triangle) bear L 'Eglingham 2¾'

👈 page 80

From Belford to Seahouses, returning over Chatton Moor

In the not too distant future, it should be possible to cross the A1 at Belford by means of a new bridge built especially for non-motorised users. This ride is split down the middle by the A1 which, being a major trunk road, has precious few safe crossing points. Fortuitously, our second crossing takes advantage of the ideally placed under-pass at North Charlton which links up directly with the lovely Hepburn Moor road. The route has two distinct characteristics: the eastern half takes advantage of the coastal plain and is almost totally devoid of any significant hills on its way to proud Bamburgh and scenic Seahouses; the western half provides a contrasting experience over glorious moorland with outstanding views of the rolling Cheviot Hills. Chillingham Castle and estate add stately grandeur and the final climb out of Chatton soon pales as the reward of exceptional coastal views is re-paid in plenty.

Start

The centre of Belford

P On the B6349, west end of Belford

Distance and grade

55 km (34 miles)

Moderate

Terrain

A long, gentle climb to Hepburn Moor with steep descent; one further climb near Chatton Park then downhill to the start. Highest point – Hepburn Moor 253 m (830 ft); Lowest point – 8 m (26 ft)

Nearest railway

Berwick-upon-Tweed, 24 km (15 miles) north of the route

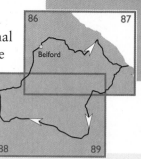

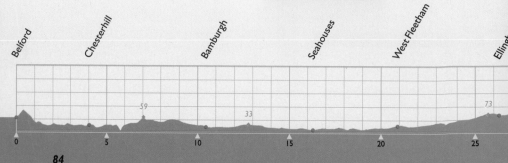

Bamburgh 4

Magnificent castle in a beautiful setting; old-fashioned village clustered round a wooded green and a stormy history spanning 14 centuries. Miles of superb beaches and sand dunes, fine views of the Farne Islands – a place to stir the imagination and well worth a longer *sojourn*. Legends abound such as the Spindleston Dragon or Laidley Worm (loathsome snake or serpent) but the heroism of Grace Darling takes pride of place; her life which was centred on Bamburgh and the Farne Islands is commemorated in the museum

Seahouses 5

Long established fishing port with busy harbour and 18th-century lime kilns, now suffering an identity crisis with the introduction of seaside amusements yet the traditional ways of 'the harvest of the sea' refuse to give way to modern trends. You can book a boat trip to see the Farne Islands which is a must; June is best but (seriously) wear warm clothes and wear a hat!

Chillingham 10

The ancestral home of the Earl of Tankerville and the 800-year home of the Chillingham Wild Cattle; sole survivors of their species remaining pure and uncrossed with any domestic cattle, always breeding white calves and totally unique

▲ Seahouses

'Singin' Hinny tea rooms, various in **Belford**
Copper Kettle tea rooms, various in **Bamburgh**
Plenty of choice in **Seahouses**
The Packhorse PH, **Ellingham**
Mason's Arms PH, Little Chef, **North Charlton**
Percy Arms PH, **Chatton**

North Charlton

Hepburn Moor

Hepburn

Chatton

253

155

118

85

8

30   35   40   45   50   54.8

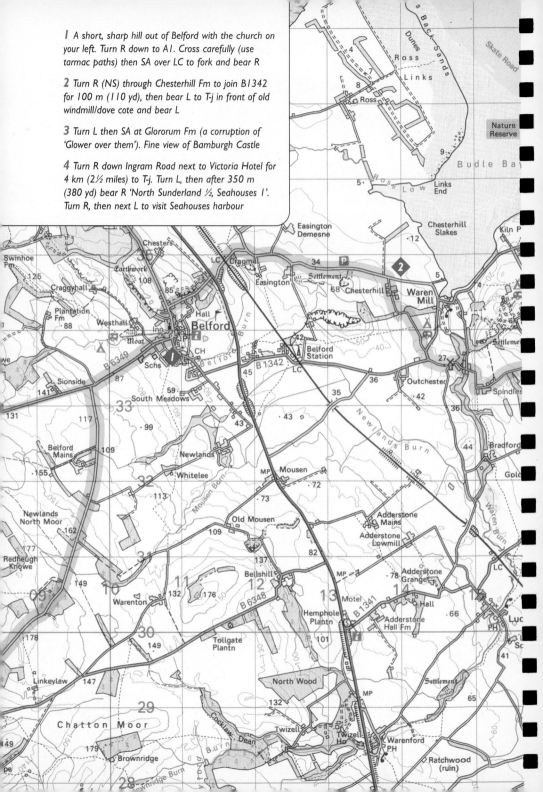

1 A short, sharp hill out of Belford with the church on your left. Turn R down to A1. Cross carefully (use tarmac paths) then SA over LC to fork and bear R

2 Turn R (NS) through Chesterhill Fm to join B1342 for 100 m (110 yd), then bear L to T-j in front of old windmill/dove cote and bear L

3 Turn L then SA at Glororum Fm (a corruption of 'Glower over them'). Fine view of Bamburgh Castle

4 Turn R down Ingram Road next to Victoria Hotel for 4 km (2½ miles) to T-j. Turn L, then after 350 m (380 yd) bear R 'North Sunderland ½, Seahouses 1'. Turn R, then next L to visit Seahouses harbour

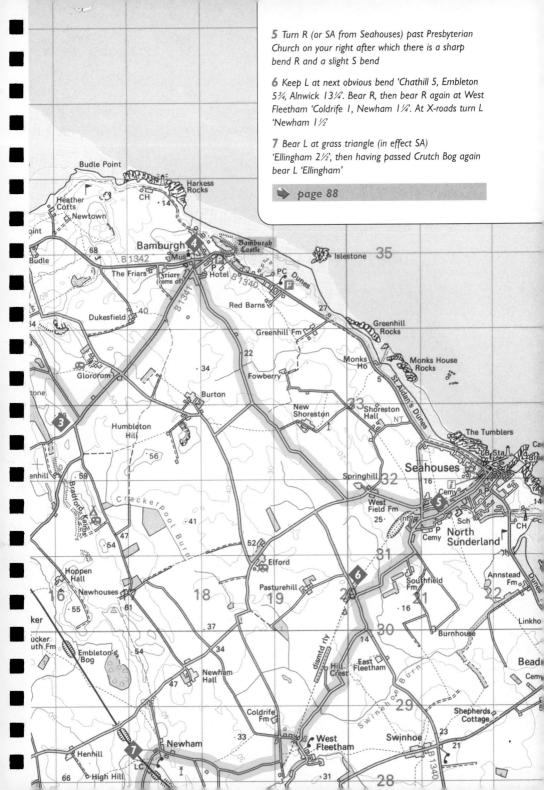

5 *Turn R (or SA from Seahouses) past Presbyterian Church on your right after which there is a sharp bend R and a slight S bend*

6 *Keep L at next obvious bend 'Chathill 5, Embleton 5¾, Alnwick 13¼'. Bear R, then bear R again at West Fleetham 'Coldrife 1, Newham 1¼'. At X-roads turn L 'Newham 1½'*

7 *Bear L at grass triangle (in effect SA) 'Ellingham 2½', then having passed Crutch Bog again bear L 'Ellingham'*

➡ page 88

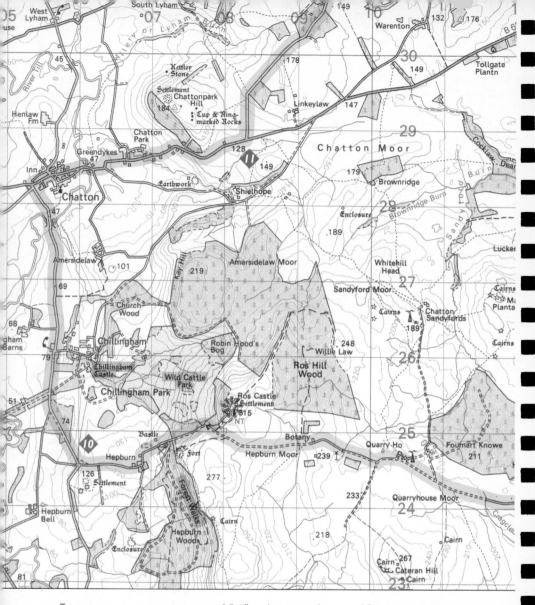

7 Bear L at grass triangle (in effect SA) 'Ellingham 2½', then having passed Crutch Bog again bear L 'Ellingham'

8 Turn R at PH (NS), then bear R 'Belford 8, Alnwick 8, North Charlton 2'. SA at X-roads 'Doxford Hall 1½ (farm vegetables sign), then bear R along private road (bridleway) to pass under the A1

9 (Turn R for refreshments.) Turn L, then R 'Chillingham' to enjoy 11 km (7 miles) of Northumberland at its best! 1:8 descent needs care.

10 Turn R past Chillingham to Chatton and turn R through village (PH). Cross bridge

11 Turn L 'Belford 4' to B6349, then turn R to return to the start

← page 86

13 *A circuit of the Kyloe Hills and a visit to Holy Island*

Belford is an ideal location for a number of excellent cycle tours which are just waiting to be enjoyed in this area. It is well placed for access to the coast as well as the fine Northumberland countryside that lies inland. This tour is relatively short but visits one of the most evocative places in the UK. After the initial climb up Belford Moor, from which the ever-present panoramic views extend in all directions, the lovely Kyloe Hills are rounded on their western flank to reach the causeway road to Lindisfarne (or Holy Island). The 'cradle of Christianity' will not disappoint and is well worth exploring but do not underestimate the time, distance and energy for the return cycle to the mainland. The now reasonably quiet section past Middleton Hall is wide and straight, being part of the old A1, and offers fine coastal views – all of which serve to make the circuit a most enjoyable experience.

 Start

The centre of Belford

🅿 On the B6349, west end of Belford

 Distance and grade

48 km (30 miles) – short distance to allow for the tide and time on the Island

✏ Easy

Terrain

Apart from the initial climb over Belford Moor, the route is either flat or downhill. Highest point – approaching Belford Moor 178 m (584 ft). Lowest point – sea level

 Nearest railway

Berwick-upon-Tweed 14 km (9 miles) from the route

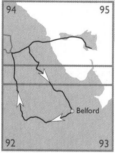

▶ *Lindisfarne Castle, Holy Island*

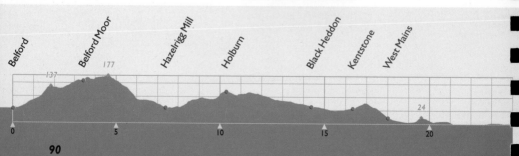

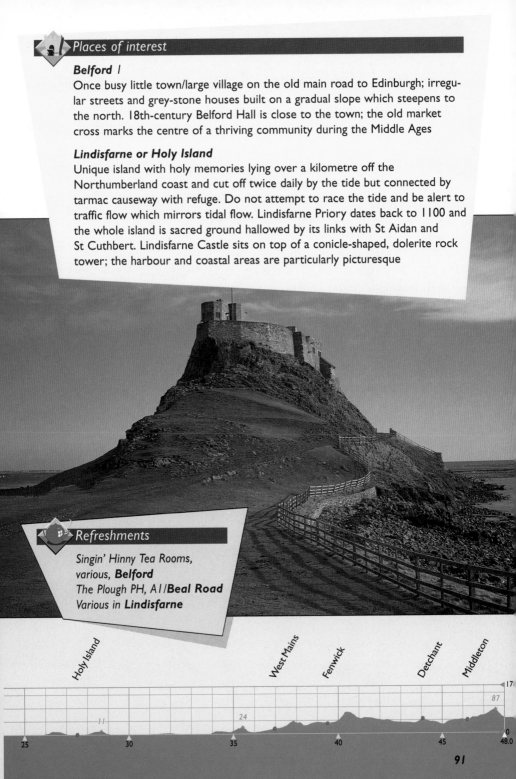

Belford 1

Once busy little town/large village on the old main road to Edinburgh; irregular streets and grey-stone houses built on a gradual slope which steepens to the north. 18th-century Belford Hall is close to the town; the old market cross marks the centre of a thriving community during the Middle Ages

Lindisfarne or Holy Island

Unique island with holy memories lying over a kilometre off the Northumberland coast and cut off twice daily by the tide but connected by tarmac causeway with refuge. Do not attempt to race the tide and be alert to traffic flow which mirrors tidal flow. Lindisfarne Priory dates back to 1100 and the whole island is sacred ground hallowed by its links with St Aidan and St Cuthbert. Lindisfarne Castle sits on top of a conicle-shaped, dolerite rock tower; the harbour and coastal areas are particularly picturesque

Refreshments

Singin' Hinny Tea Rooms,
various, **Belford**
The Plough PH, A1/**Beal Road**
Various in **Lindisfarne**

Holy Island   West Mains   Fenwick   Derchant   Middleton

11   24   87   17

25   30   35   40   45   48.0

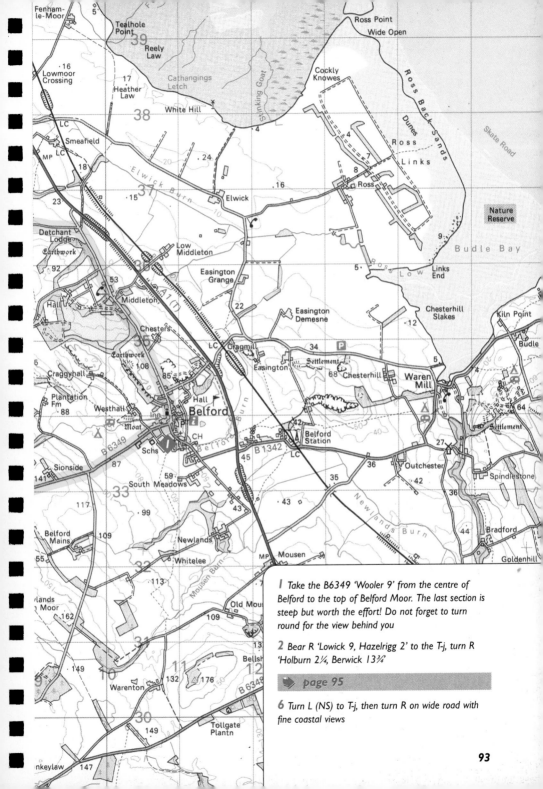

1 Take the B6349 'Wooler 9' from the centre of Belford to the top of Belford Moor. The last section is steep but worth the effort! Do not forget to turn round for the view behind you

2 Bear R 'Lowick 9, Hazelrigg 2' to the T-j, turn R 'Holburn 2¼, Berwick 13¾'

⇨ page 95

6 Turn L (NS) to T-j, then turn R on wide road with fine coastal views

3 At B6353 X-roads SA to T-j, then turn R 'Kentstone, Beal' to A1 (**Or** for link to on-road Route 14 SA at X-roads and turn L at T-j, then bear R to join Route 14 between instructions 4/5)

4 Cross carefully, then turn R. Turn L along short section of old road past the garage for a further 50 m (55 yd) using the wide grass verge

until opposite the minor road **NB** new crossing point planned. Cross carefully, then narrow road to B6353. (**Or** SA, tide tables on the left, shop at garage and PH **NB** The causeway access road can be busy as the traffic flows in time with the tide)

A *Take care*. Check the tide times before crossing and

allow plenty of time. Remember your return across the causeway may be against a headwind. Retrace to instruction 4

5 Bear L then bear R at Fenwick leading to a short, sharp hill. Bear L to free-wheel almost all of the way to Detchant

◀ page 93

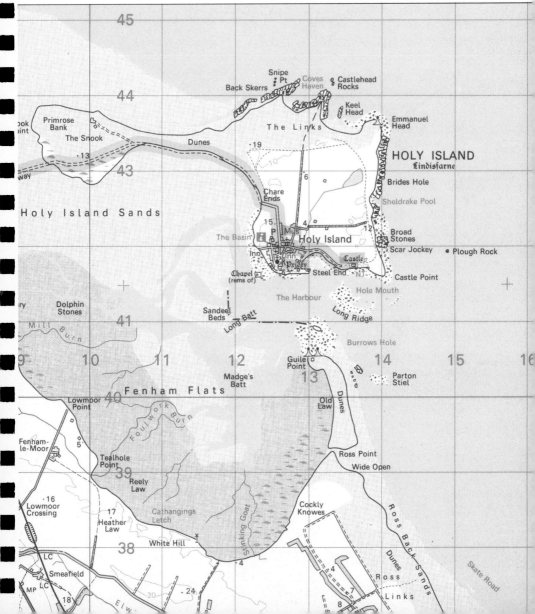

North of Wooler to the Scottish Border, returning by Ford and Etal

The nearer you get to the Scottish border, the more grid-shaped the roads become. This has both good and bad points depending on the road classification and associated traffic flow; this ride takes advantage of two of the several right-angle crossings of the fast and straight A698 Coldstream to Berwick road which exist as a result of the grid. Starting at the attractive market town of Wooler and leaving the Cheviot Hills behind, this route crosses the eye-catching Weetwood Bridge to climb up and around Horton Moor. The straight but nevertheless interesting line of the Devil's Causeway (old Roman road) is followed to Lowick after which several alternatives present themselves: west to Duddo; east to Holy Island or on, via Ancroft, to Norham on the Scottish border. The return route takes in the lovely communities of Etal, Heatherslaw Mill and Ford, where a certain timeless charm pervades the air, before continuing south towards Doddington and back to your starting point.

Start

High Street, Wooler

P Padgepool Place, west of Wooler High Street

Distance and grade

66 km (39 miles) – short route 44 km (26½ miles)

Easy/moderate

Terrain

Gently undulating with only one significant climb of 91 m over 5 km (300 ft over 3 miles). Highest point – Horton Moor 141 m (463 ft). Lowest point – near Norham 7 m (23 ft)

Nearest railway

Berwick-upon-Tweed, 7 km (4 miles) north-east of the route

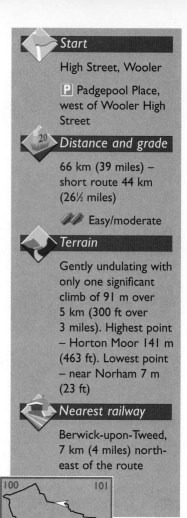

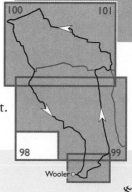

Norham 8

A remarkable Tweedside village with one long street of grey stone cottages and a triangular green with a quaint pinnacled market cross set on a base of 6 13th-century steps. Large church going back to AD 830; splendid but shattered walls of the castle and keep tower above the river and the village – worthy of a visit and further research

Etal, Heatherslaw and Ford 9/10

Tiny Etal is utterly charming with thatched cottages and pub; an imposing 14th-century castle lies close to the banks of the River Till. Nearby Heatherslaw Mill is a working demonstration mill complete with narrow guage railway. Ford is a model village with a castle dating back to 1282 and a 13th-century church close by

Refreshments

Plenty of choice in **Wooler**
White Swan PH, shop, **Lowick**
The Lamb PH, **Ancroft**
The Plough PH, **West Allerdean**
Various in **Norham**
Black Bull, shop, **Etal**
Tea rooms, **Heatherslaw Mill**

▼ River Till near Doddington Bridge

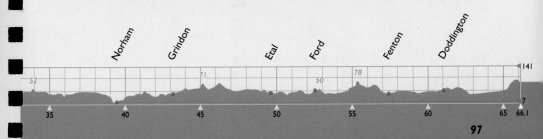

97

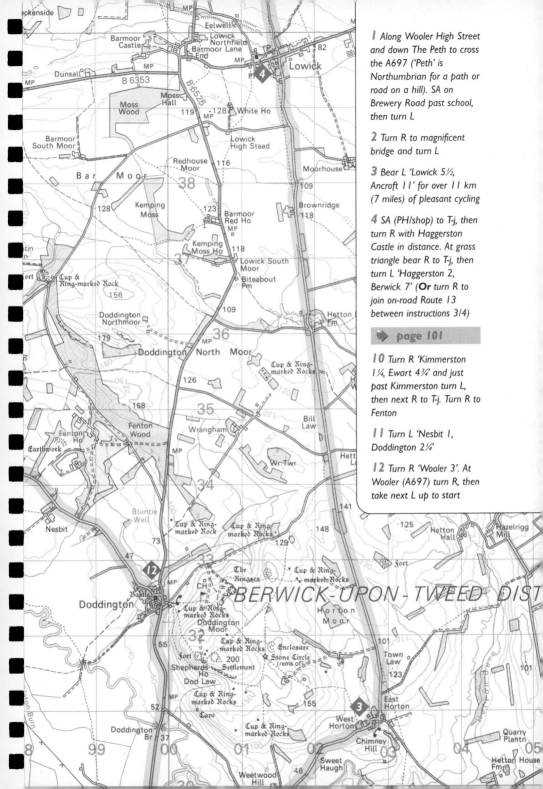

1 Along Wooler High Street and down The Peth to cross the A697 ('Peth' is Northumbrian for a path or road on a hill). SA on Brewery Road past school, then turn L

2 Turn R to magnificent bridge and turn L

3 Bear L 'Lowick 5½, Ancroft 11' for over 11 km (7 miles) of pleasant cycling

4 SA (PH/shop) to T-j, then turn R with Haggerston Castle in distance. At grass triangle bear R to T-j, then turn L 'Haggerston 2, Berwick 7' (**Or** turn R to join on-road Route 13 between instructions 3/4)

➡ page 101

10 Turn R 'Kimmerston 1¼, Ewart 4¾' and just past Kimmerston turn L, then next R to T-j. Turn R to Fenton

11 Turn L 'Nesbit 1, Doddington 2¼'

12 Turn R 'Wooler 3'. At Wooler (A697) turn R, then take next L up to start

4 SA (PH/shop) to T-j, then turn R with Haggerston Castle in distance. At grass triangle bear R to T-j, then turn L 'Haggerston 2, Berwick 7' (**Or** turn R to join on-road Route 13 between instructions 3/4)

1 Short cut

From instruction 4 SA to T-j, then turn L to B6525; turn R, then after 500 m (545 yd) turn L through Bowsden. Fork L (do not confuse with previous L turn) to B6354, then turn L to join instruction 9

5 Turn L 'Haggerston, Scremerston', then after just over 1 km turn L 'Ancroft 2' through New Haggerston Fm. At next T-j turn R 'Cheswick 1½, Ancroft 1¾', then at Ancroft Mill turn L 'Ancroft 2'

6 Turn R. (PH) turn L (in effect SA) and bear R at Allerdean Grange corner past neat hedges to off-set X-roads (PH). Turn L, then R (in effect SA)

7 Turn R (NS but opposite Shoresdean), then turn next L (NS). Bear R to A698, then turn R for 300 m (328 yd) and turn L (in effect SA) past railway bridge

8 Through Norham, then at far end of village turn L on B6470 for 800 m (½ mile). 'Norham Station ¼, Cornhill 6'. Turn L, then turn R to cross A698

9 Keep L, then turn R 'Duddo 2, Etal 4, Ford 6½'. SA at next X-roads to B6354, turn R to visit Etal (PH), Heatherslaw Mill (refreshments) and Ford

◀ page 99

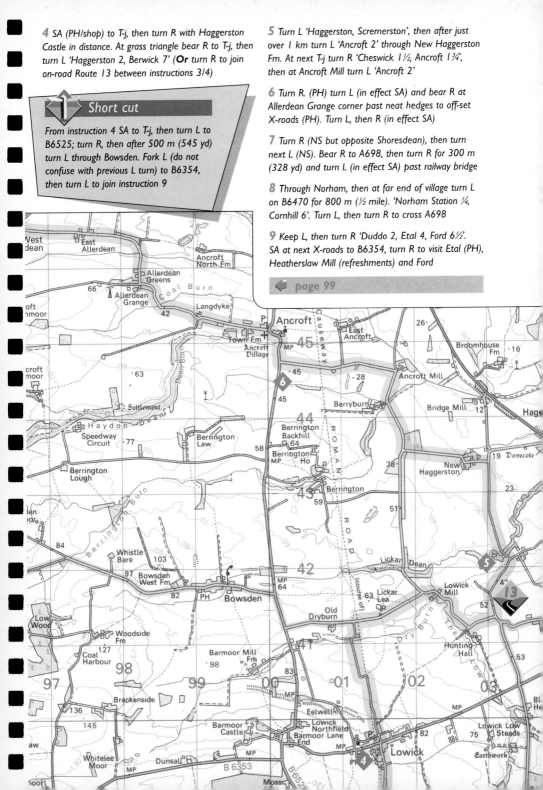

A circuit from Bishop Auckland on railway paths, and quiet lanes

At the present time there are some 120 km (75 miles) of converted railway paths in County Durham with proposals for more to be added when finance becomes available. This ride follows two separate but converging railway paths, a very pleasant minor road and a section of linking bridleways – most of which are situated in a truly rural setting. The ride starts and finishes at Bishop Auckland for convenience but can be joined at any point. The Auckland Walk links with Spennymoor of which little is seen. The ensuing bridleways add an interesting off-road aspect to the circuit then a quiet, minor road leads to the Brandon/Bishop Auckland Walk. Finally, the Newton Cap Viaduct provides the high-level river crossing to return to the start.

Start

Bishop Auckland, near Auckland Castle

P Parking by the river at Bishop Auckland (GR 213303); short steep hill (Wear Chare) – take care joining the route

Distance and grade

29 km (18 miles)

🖊 Easy

Terrain

All the railway paths are level and there is only one real hill on the entire route in the shape of a steady haul on the A689 to join the Auckland Walk railway path. Highest point – A689/railway path 141 m (463 ft). Lowest point – Sunderland Bridge 38 m (125 ft)

Nearest railway

Bishop Auckland

Refreshments

Plenty of choice in **Bishop Auckland**
Various off the route in **Spennymoor**
Various off the route in **Brandon**
Various in **Willington**

▲ *Brancepeth Castle near Brandon*

Places of interest

Bishop Auckland 1
Small town of local importance with a mixture of old and new architecture; Auckland Castle had humble beginnings as a manor house but was converted into a castle in about 1300 which was the start of a long process of enlargements and alterations designed to beautify the place. Much was destroyed by fire in the 1650s and largely restored 10 years later; the residence of the Bishop of Durham since Norman times

Byers Green, Whitworth Hall *and* Bracepeth Castle
Byers Green Station (2) can still be seen; 'byers' means ancient woods which grew around the village. Whitworth Hall (west of 4) was once the home of the musical legend, Bobby Shaftoe. Brancepeth Castle (southwest of 10), much restored in the 19th century, was originally a 13th-century castle built by the Nevill family to replace a Saxon stronghold

Binchester 2/3
Roman military station on the Dere Street known as 'Vinovia' which means pleasant place; the hypercaust is the best example of a Roman bath house in Britain. NB Off-route, but a picturesque, minor road along the River Wear will add pleasure to a worthwhile detour

Scripton   Brancepeth   Willington

119   124   89   141
99

15   20   25   28.7

38

1 Ascend Wear Chare, then turn L to pass the main entrance to Auckland Castle on your left. Descend A689 all too briefly, then ascend all too slowly to railway path which passes under the road

2 Descend to railway path on south side of road, then turn L

3 Turn L, then next R to Tudhoe Grange Estate. Turn L to corner of estate

4 Bear R keeping houses on your right and follow path through wood, down to stream

5 Cross concrete bridge, then up and around L to minor road, turn R

6 Turn L, then sharp R (bridleway) to farm track. SA along field edge (narrow) to corner of wood

7 Enter wood (tricky) and follow path (can be muddy) down to stream (awkward bridge)

8 Keep river on your left and follow improving track to old Sunderland Bridge. Turn L, then sharp L along obvious track keeping river on your left

9 Bear L to join minor road, then turn R to A690. Turn R, then sharp L to railway path

10 Turn L and follow railway path to Newton Cap Viaduct (A689/Bishop Auckland)

11 Cross bridge using footpath, then turn L to return to the start

2 *East of Washington around Penshaw Monument*

One of the possible destinations of the C2C Cycle Route is Sunderland and this ride uses its west/east axis, albeit in the opposite direction, to form the longest side of the circuit. Surrounded by conurbations, this surprisingly rural ride can be joined at any point but starts near Rickleton for convenience. A bridleway leads close to Lambton Castle then links with light-controlled Biddick Bridge across the river Wear before passing under the A182 and through Biddick Woods via Boundary Houses and south of Success to Philadelphia and on to New Herrington. Bridleways connect West and Middle Herrington after which Foxcover Road leads to Offerton Lane and the C2C route. Cox Green pedestrian bridge gives pleasant access to North Biddick and leaving the excellent railway path at Vigo Wood the path through Rickleton completes the enjoyably rural circuit of Penshaw Monument.

Start

Bonemill Lane, near Rickleton (GR 294537)

[P] Parking at the Sports Ground midway along the south side of the road between Rickleton and Fatfield (Bonemill Lane)

Distance and grade

22 km (14 miles)

🔋 Easy

Terrain

Only one short uphill approaching instruction 7 but there are several good descents. Do the ride clockwise if you want more exercise! Highest point – approaching instruction 7 109 m (358 ft). Lowest point – sea level

Nearest railway

Chester-le-Street, 4 km (2 miles) southwest of the start

Refreshments

*Plenty of choice in **Biddock area**
Shoulder of Mutton PH, **West Herrington**
Oddfellows Arms PH, **Cox Green***

Rickleton · Biddick Hall · Shiney Row · New Herrington · Middle Herring...

35   17   69

0   5   10

Cox Green 10

The village of Cox Green and the settlement of Barmston on the opposite bank of the river shared three boat-building yards; two slipways are still visible. In days gone by the main industries were boat-building, quarrying and river work; prior to 1955 a wire rope and rowing boat were the only means of crossing the river until the present bridge was built in 1958. Upstream from the bridge (south side) is Alice's Well which still produces spring water; this was the only souce of drinking water until World War 2

Penshaw Monument 5

In 1840, it was decided to build a monument to the memory of the Earl of Durham who had just died. Penshaw Hill was selected and Penshaw Monument was built in the design of a Grecian temple based on the temple of Theseus. Watched by a crowd of over 10,000 people, the foundation stone was laid in 1844; the 21.3 m (70 ft) high monument, which is a highly visible landmark, is now owned by the National Trust. Its main claim to fame is that the legendary Lambton Worm wrapped its tail '10 times round Penshaw Hill'

▲ *Washington Old Hall, Washington*

1 Leave Bonemill Lane with the Sports Fields on your right (bridleway). Follow tarmac road under A182, then on to cross Biddick Bridge

2 Turn R down cul-de-sac between houses (bridleway) to pass under the A182

3 Cross over to tarmac path and turn L over bridge. Take next turn R after 30 mph sign (Briar Lea), then at T-j turn L (Bowes Lea). Take 2nd turn R, then through corner gap to access sports field and the road beyond. Turn R

4 Turn L alongside disused railway line to Philadelphia. Turn R, then sharp L **NB** old converted engine sheds. Through gap, then turn R (bridleway) keeping grass on your left. **NB** Site of Dorothea Pit

5 Under bridge, then onto tarmac road on right of railway path to sharp turn R by double row of red brick houses to West Herrington

6 SA with PH on the left to cross A19 (bridge), then turn L along Foxcover Road

7 SA, then turn R through Offerton and follow Offerton Lane parallel to, but separate from, the A19

8 Join Consett and Sunderland Railway Path (C2C) and turn L

9 Turn R down to River Wear, then turn L to cross bridge **NB** Alice Well in wall 30 m (33 yd) beyond bridge (south side)

10 Turn L (grass), then at 2nd seat turn R (clump of trees) past metal barrier to tarmac road and turn L to Jubilee Terrace. Turn R at near end (bridleway, 'Pattinson Pond'). Follow C2C Route signs in reverse. After next barrier turn L for 500 m (545 yd), then bear L under railway. **Easy to miss.** Immediate turn R to main railway path beyond burgundy coloured access control point

11 Bear L along Consett and Sunderland Railway Path crossing A182 to turn off L, midway between 2 sets of meter-high posts (red), in middle of track

12 Turn R on estate road to far end of houses. Turn L (Woodland Trust sign) and push your bike along the tarmac path to cross road at Rickleton Chapel to access sports field. Turn R and push your bike along the tarmac path until it passes under Bonemill Lane to the return to the start

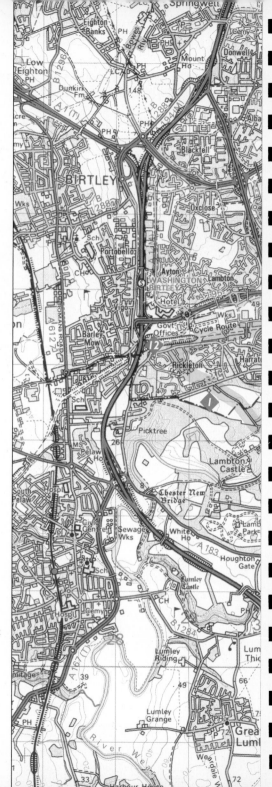

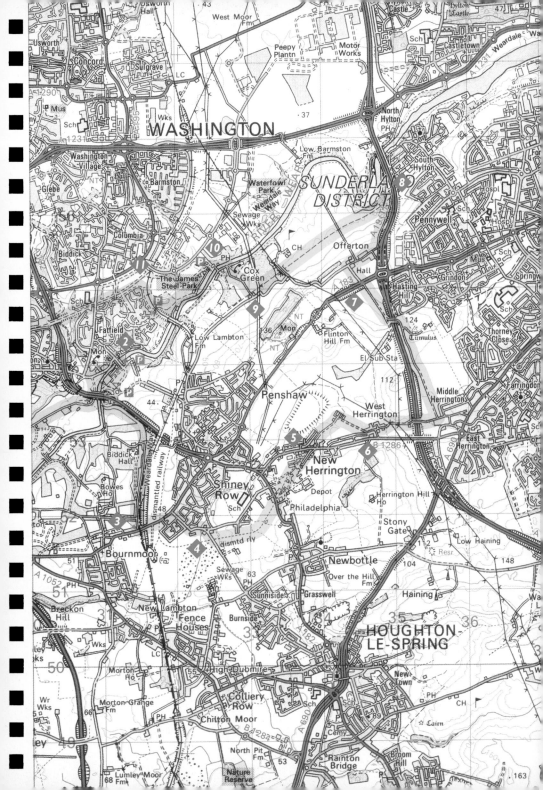

3 Along the Tyne from Prudhoe then southwest from Wylam

Commencing at the Tyne Riverside Country Park, this route shares a short but enjoyable section of on-road Route 3 between Prudhoe and Wylam before heading up and away from the riverside to cross the A695 and continue along very pleasant lanes to cross the Stanley Burn back into Northumberland. Once the Dukeshagg Bank is surmounted, the minor road beyond descends to connect with a very interesting bridleway heading west to a point where the route splits. The shorter option offers extremely rewarding views over Stocksfield Burn towards Broomley and Healey and the longer option provides an enjoyable and easy, rural ride. Both options merge at New Ridley just in time for the ascension to High Mickley. The descent via Cherryburn links up with a delightful lane which leads back to the A695 and the final descent to the country park.

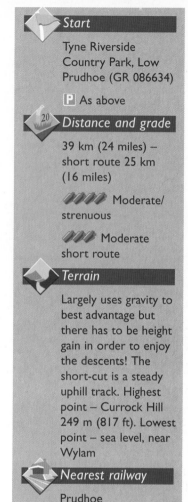

Start

Tyne Riverside Country Park, Low Prudhoe (GR 086634)

P As above

Distance and grade

39 km (24 miles) – short route 25 km (16 miles)

🍀🍀🍀 Moderate/strenuous

🍀🍀🍀 Moderate short route

Terrain

Largely uses gravity to best advantage but there has to be height gain in order to enjoy the descents! The short-cut is a steady uphill track. Highest point – Currock Hill 249 m (817 ft). Lowest point – sea level, near Wylam

Nearest railway

Prudhoe

Prudhoe Castle /

Pronounced 'Pruda' and proudly standing on high ground to the south of the River Tyne. Built in late Norman times by Ordinel de Umfraville, probably on the site of a wooden stronghold, became the property of the Percys some 150 years later. A magnificent castle with an interesting history and well worth a visit

The Spetchells /

Lying next to the cycle path are the Spetchells which are long, large heaps of white lime. Originally stockpiled for later distribution to farms for the purpose of neutralising acidic land, thus encouraging optimum growth potential, the heaps have become well established landmarks

Refreshments

PH, **Prudhoe**
Bridge End PH, White Swan PH, **Ovingham**
Various in **Wylam**
The Anchor PH 🍺,
Whittonstall
Dr Syntax PH,
New Ridley
The Bluebell PH, **Low Mickley** (off-route)
Jiggery Pokery tea rooms **Mickley Square**

◀ George Stephenson's Cottage, Wylam

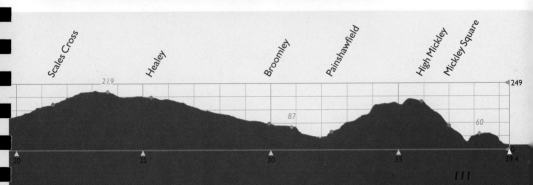

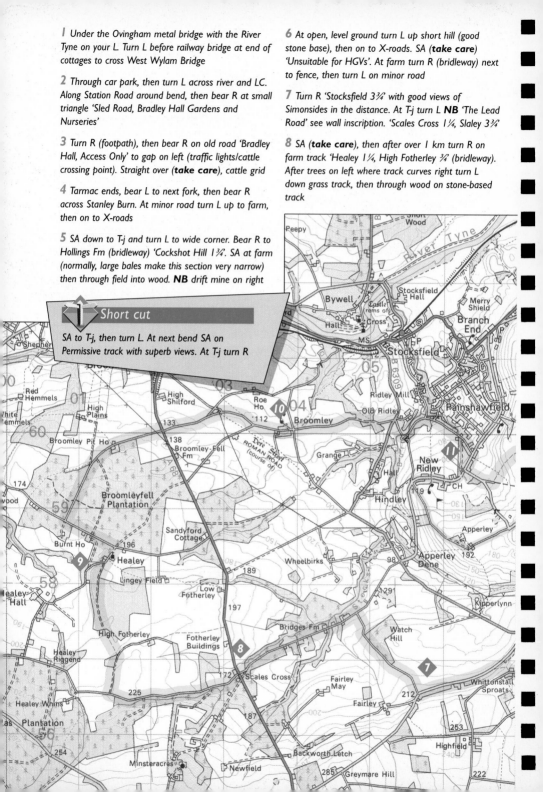

1 Under the Ovingham metal bridge with the River Tyne on your L. Turn L before railway bridge at end of cottages to cross West Wylam Bridge

2 Through car park, then turn L across river and LC. Along Station Road around bend, then bear R at small triangle 'Sled Road, Bradley Hall Gardens and Nurseries'

3 Turn R (footpath), then bear R on old road 'Bradley Hall, Access Only' to gap on left (traffic lights/cattle crossing point). Straight over (**take care**), cattle grid

4 Tarmac ends, bear L to next fork, then bear R across Stanley Burn. At minor road turn L up to farm, then on to X-roads

5 SA down to T-j and turn L to wide corner. Bear R to Hollings Fm (bridleway) 'Cockshot Hill 1¾'. SA at farm (normally, large bales make this section very narrow) then through field into wood. **NB** drift mine on right

6 At open, level ground turn L up short hill (good stone base), then on to X-roads. SA (**take care**) 'Unsuitable for HGVs'. At farm turn R (bridleway) next to fence, then turn L on minor road

7 Turn R 'Stocksfield 3¾' with good views of Simonsides in the distance. At T-j turn L **NB** 'The Lead Road' see wall inscription. 'Scales Cross 1¼, Slaley 3¾'

8 SA (**take care**), then after over 1 km turn R on farm track 'Healey 1¼, High Fotherley ¾' (bridleway). After trees on left where track curves right turn L down grass track, then through wood on stone-based track

Short cut

SA to T-j, then turn L. At next bend SA on Permissive track with superb views. At T-j turn R

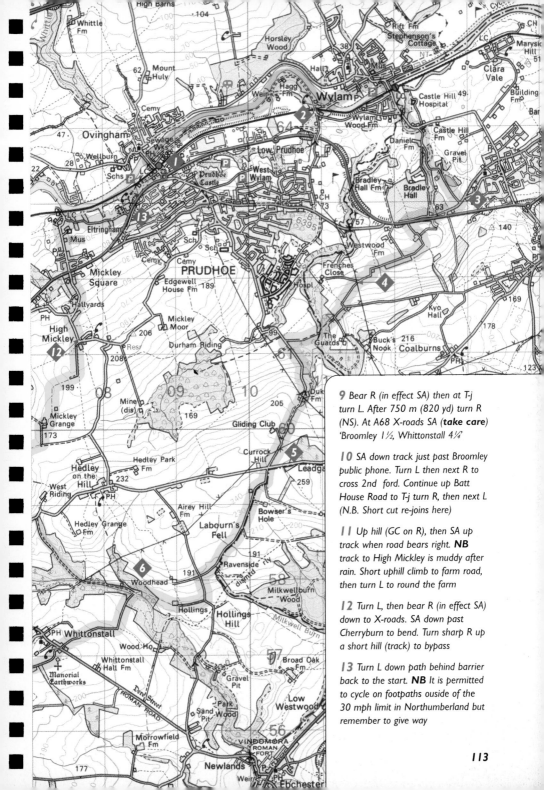

9 Bear R (in effect SA) then at T-j turn L. After 750 m (820 yd) turn R (NS). At A68 X-roads SA (**take care**) 'Broomley 1½, Whittonstall 4¼'

10 SA down track just past Broomley public phone. Turn L then next R to cross 2nd ford. Continue up Batt House Road to T-j turn R, then next L (N.B. Short cut re-joins here)

11 Up hill (GC on R), then SA up track when road bears right. **NB** track to High Mickley is muddy after rain. Short uphill climb to farm road, then turn L to round the farm

12 Turn L, then bear R (in effect SA) down to X-roads. SA down past Cherryburn to bend. Turn sharp R up a short hill (track) to bypass

13 Turn L down path behind barrier back to the start. **NB** It is permitted to cycle on footpaths ouside of the 30 mph limit in Northumberland but remember to give way

4 Across fells north of Bellingham and east to Linnheads Lake

Start

Main Street,
Bellingham
(GR 839834)

P As above or on left
beyond public toilets

Distance and grade

42 km (26 miles) –
short route 24 km
(15 miles)

Strenuous

*Moderate/
strenuous short route*

Terrain

A complete mix of
terrain and surfaces; an
amalgam of all that is
good and challenging in
an off-road ride. In
general the spectacular
downs far outweigh
the necessary ups.

This ride is an energetic excursion over a great variety of terrain. After gradually gaining height above Bellingham the Pennine Way bridleway is followed as far as the quiet B6320 but the surface varies and requires care – during or after wet weather the on-road alternative is recommended. Choose a clear day to enjoy the wonderful views during the superb descent from Corsenside Common, now rarely used by the military. Two little-known bridges are revealed by dint of rarely-used Unclassified County Roads (UCRs) and are the 'hidden secrets' of the ride. East Woodburn Common leads past picturesque Linnheads Lake and then very pleasantly through the forest to access a short stretch of fell. The return route, threading past Sweethope Loughs, takes advantage of narrow tarmac with no shortage of views. There is an optional off-road link for those with boundless energy and rear suspension and the final loop, north of Redesmouth, should not be missed.

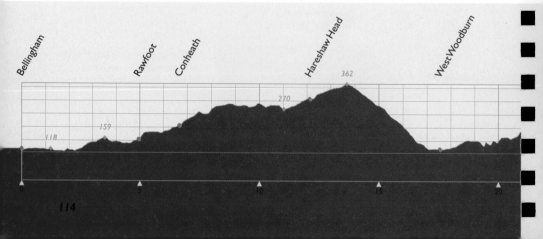

Highest point –
Corsenside Common
364 m (1194 ft).
Lowest point – Rede
Bridge 107 m (353 ft)

Nearest railway

Corbridge, 20 km
(12 miles) south of the
route

▲ *The Bellingham Gingall*

Refreshments

*Various, cafe and tea
rooms,* **Bellingham**
Bay Horse, shop,
West Woodburn

Places of interest

West Woodburn 9

Small village on the A68 close to the
great Roman road Dere Street. The
route ran from York to Hadrian's Wall
then continued northwards, actually
crossing the River Rede at the end of
instruction 8. Some of the stones
in the river were part of the original
bridge, built when the river used to
flood and became a lake before
upstream Catcleugh
Reservoir dam was con-
structed. Until AD 140 the
bridgehead was a small
island in the middle of a
swamp when the Romans
decided to build a fort
called Habitancum now
known as Risingham.
Abandoned in about AD
367, the fort lay untouched
until 1822 when the site
was bought by the Shanks
family who John Hodgson,
the vicar and local historian,
later encouraged to excavate. In 1839
John Shanks unearthed a cement-lined
bath which was then destroyed to dis-
courage sightseers. Certain valuable
finds were sent to Newcastle including
the altar of local god Magons, and a
4th-century Christian tombstone

Hartside

Sweethope Loughs

Green Rigg

Buteland Fell

Rede Bridge

364

279

289

227

200

141

111

107

25

30

35

40

41.9

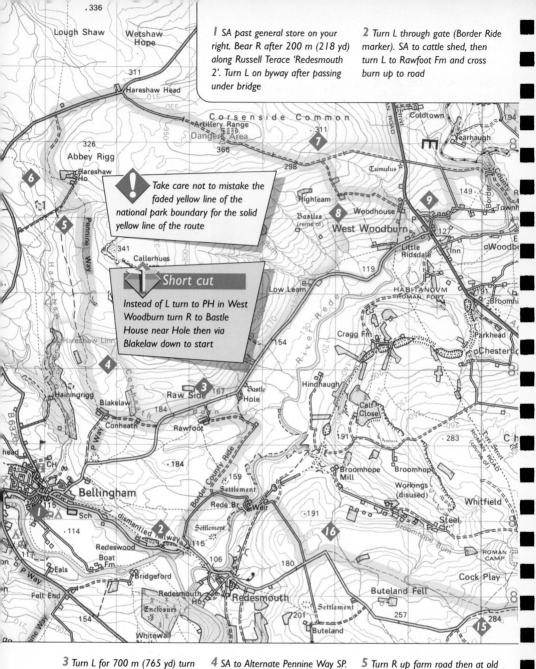

1 SA past general store on your right. Bear R after 200 m (218 yd) along Russell Terace 'Redesmouth 2'. Turn L on byway after passing under bridge

2 Turn L through gate (Border Ride marker). SA to cattle shed, then turn L to Rawfoot Fm and cross burn up to road

! Take care not to mistake the faded yellow line of the national park boundary for the solid yellow line of the route

1 Short cut

Instead of L turn to PH in West Woodburn turn R to Bastle House near Hole then via Blakelaw down to start

3 Turn L for 700 m (765 yd) turn R to Blakelaw Fm. SA on Pennine Way through farm to post on near horizon. SA to corner of wall, then up to post on next horizon – on the right of trees (gate)

4 SA to Alternate Pennine Way SP. Legal route takes R fork over a number of drainage ditches to wall by Scotch Pine, no gate. Turn L down wall to bottom gate, to meet Alternate Pennine Way

5 Turn R up farm road then at old building turn L (full gate, bridleway sign). Traverse (full gate) to red stream (iron deposits), bear R through gate and SA on double width track (old wagonway)

6 Turn R on B6320 to farm, then turn R again (public road – rarely closed for firing)

7 After descending past 2nd set of red warning signs on gate look for half bend in road then, after 200 m (218 yd), turn R (gate/stone posts) onto double rough track, downhill to farm

8 At gate keep L around farm to tarmac road (bridleway). Descend to Woodhouse. Turn R through gate past metal barn on double track to road. Turn L to PH in West Woodburn

9 15 m (16 yd) beyond PH (wide path) turn R, then L after 600 m (656 yd) up to corner. At gate turn R to Blackburn Bridge. Turn R

10 SA (gate) to double track. Track bends on up to gap in rocky skyline (with a quarry behind)

11 After 25 m (27 yd) bear R keeping wall on your right. Through end gate, keeping wall on left, to red track. SA across track, then after 150 m (165 yd) continue diagonally down to follow track into wood, lake on right

12 Bear R (look for small quarry on left). **Easy to miss**. Down to bend but SA on forest ride (fire gap) to bridle gate and to fell – walk this section

13 Follow fence, then cut diagonally down to old Wanney railway line – keep well left of small hut, through tunnel (near to trees) then up steeply (ridable!) and across to road

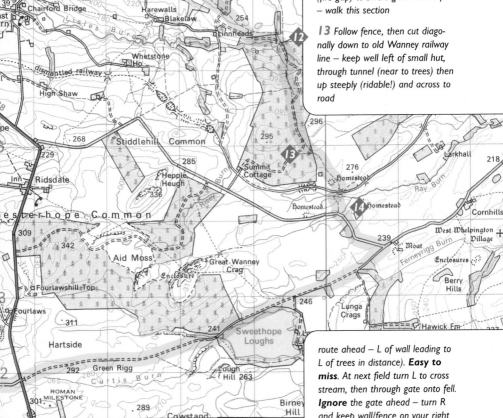

14 Turn L, then next R past lake **take care** – listen for following traffic – to A68 X-roads. SA (**take care**) 700 m (765 yd) to gate on right, just past small quarry on left. Continue SA on-road

to instruction 15 (and on-road to instruction 16 to miss next bumpy off-road section)

15 **Easy to miss**. Turn R on feint track to brow, then downhill (sight

route ahead – L of wall leading to L of trees in distance). **Easy to miss**. At next field turn L to cross stream, then through gate onto fell. **Ignore** the gate ahead – turn R and keep wall/fence on your right past wood. Continue diagonally to corner of field and onto road

16 SA, then R, after 300 m (330 yd) turn R down to Rede Bridge, then up to reverse first section back to the start

5 Weaving along the Wansbeck, west of Morpeth

The wild and windy Wanneys lie to the west of this route and are a truly craggy domain. The Wansbeck has its source close by before it curls its way eastwards on a relatively short jouney to the sea. There are a total of eight river crossings on this ride not counting the numerous burns or streams – the River Wansbeck alone is crossed five times over the first 9 km (5½ miles). The rivers Wansbeck, Font and Hart Burn have all joined forces by Mitford but the map-bleary cyclist may be prone to river confusion as the ride progresses. The route weaves its way around numerous hamlets, all whilst threading its way back and forth across the various water courses. By this means, and the use of rarely-used unclassified County roads now little more than tracks, the route will take you into some of Northumberland's loveliest places. A network of quiet lanes leads easily and gently onto higher ground from which you

Start

Morpeth (GR 189862)

P Morpeth, River Wansbeck Country Park on B6343 (GR 189862)

Distance and grade

46 km (29 miles)

Easy/moderate

Terrain

Scenic tour of green fields and rivers, hamlets and woods by country lanes and tracks. The only real exertion will come from cycling over bumpy ground. Highest point – near Rayburn Lake and 172 m (564 ft). Lowest point – Morpeth 26 m (86 ft)

Nearest railway

Morpeth

can see the distant Simonside and Cheviot Hills. Beckon though they will, 'weaving along the Wansbeck' is the treat that this ride has in store.

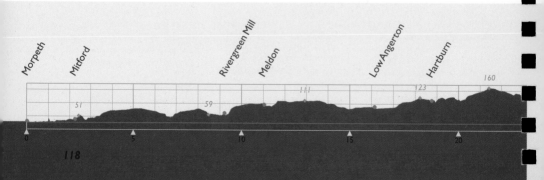

Morpeth · Mitford · Rivergreen Mill · Meldon · Low Angerton · Hartburn

51 · 59 · 111 · 123 · 160

0 · 5 · 10 · 15 · 20

Morpeth and the Wansbeck Valley

Further to this chapter's introduction, a historical perspective can add to the appreciation of the true Wansbeck Valley which extends about 3 km (2 miles) between Morpeth and Mitford. About 2 km (1½ miles) from Morpeth is Newminster Abbey of which very little remains; it was almost identical to Fountains Abbey in Yorkshire and was founded by Cistercian monks in 1137. The estate was extensive, stretching from the source of the Wansbeck, up Coquetdale with fisheries on the Tyne and saltworks at the mouth of both the Blyth and the Coquet. High Stanners was named after the small stones and gravel on the margins of the river; Low Stanners was formerly a place of execution on the eastern outskirts of the town. Lady's Walk leads to Newminster and refers to the Virgin Mother; Lover's Walk ends in the sheltered haugh below the ruins

▶ Refreshments

Plenty of choice in **Morpeth**
The Plough PH, **Mitford**
The Dyke Neuk PH,
north of instruction 5

▲ Morpeth Embankment on the River Wansbeck

Devil's Causeway — Netherwitton — Doe Hill Farm — Stanton — Pigdon — Mitford

1 Cross bridge on B6343, then along to Mitford (PH)

2 Turn L 'Mitford ¼, Mitford Steads 1, Molesden 2½'

3 Turn R (in effect SA) along double track down to stepping stones and on up to B6343. Turn L, then after 1 km turn L down track – **easy to miss** – 200 m (218 yd) **before** next farm on your right and follow track down to, and then alongside, the River Wansbeck

4 Cross narrow bridge, then up short, steep hill to minor road. Bear R to grass triangle

5 Turn L through Meldon. After old church on left bear R to cross old railway bridge to T-j, then turn R

6 Turn R through gate past Howlett Hall Fm, then sharp L to Low Angerton

7 SA, then through bridle gate on L (railway sleeper gatepost) just past wood on right. **NB** 'Causeway' across potential flood plain on right. Pass mature wood on right and cross field to gate with white Countryside Access sign (next to young wood on left). Turn R with fence on your right. Continue gently up to gate, then SA (easier) to road

8 SA 'Hartburn ¾', then bear R to Hartburn. Turn L at the cross

9 Turn R (in effect SA) over cattle grid, to cross River Wansbeck, then after 50 m (55 yd) bear R along narrow path/jungle (bridleway muddy after rain). Cross small stream (narrow bridge) and push up short, steep hill. Follow field edge to a better path near farm

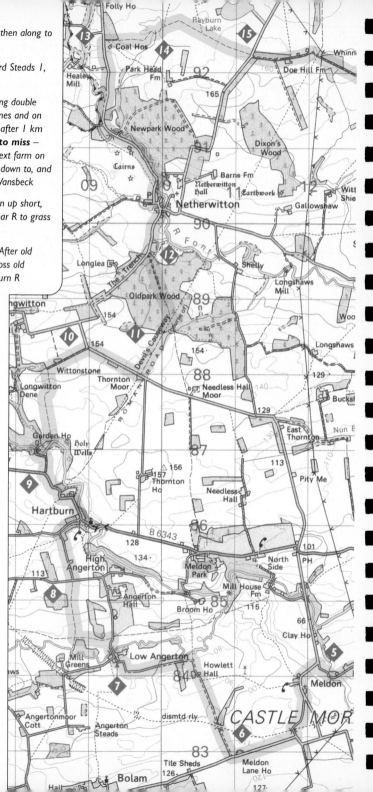

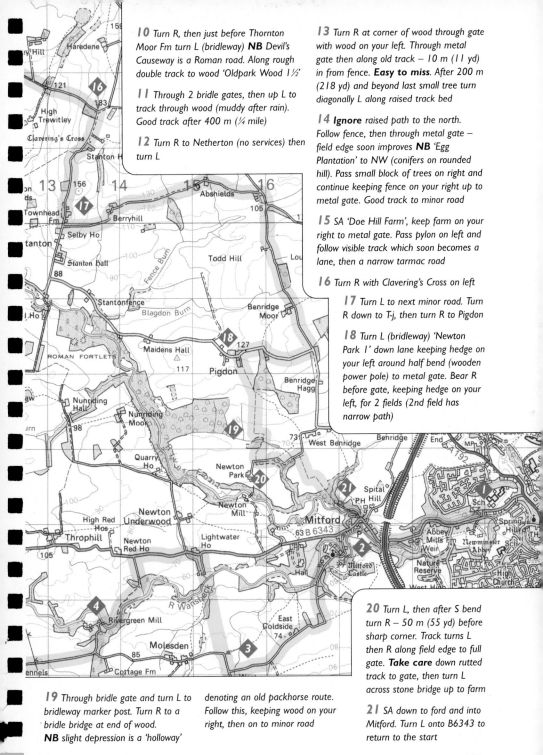

10 Turn R, then just before Thornton Moor Fm turn L (bridleway) **NB** Devil's Causeway is a Roman road. Along rough double track to wood 'Oldpark Wood 1½'

11 Through 2 bridle gates, then up L to track through wood (muddy after rain). Good track after 400 m (¼ mile)

12 Turn R to Netherton (no services) then turn L

13 Turn R at corner of wood through gate with wood on your left. Through metal gate then along old track – 10 m (11 yd) in from fence. **Easy to miss**. After 200 m (218 yd) and beyond last small tree turn diagonally L along raised track bed

14 Ignore raised path to the north. Follow fence, then through metal gate – field edge soon improves **NB** 'Egg Plantation' to NW (conifers on rounded hill). Pass small block of trees on right and continue keeping fence on your right up to metal gate. Good track to minor road

15 SA 'Doe Hill Farm', keep farm on your right to metal gate. Pass pylon on left and follow visible track which soon becomes a lane, then a narrow tarmac road

16 Turn R with Clavering's Cross on left

17 Turn L to next minor road. Turn R down to T-j, then turn R to Pigdon

18 Turn L (bridleway) 'Newton Park 1' down lane keeping hedge on your left around half bend (wooden power pole) to metal gate. Bear R before gate, keeping hedge on your left, for 2 fields (2nd field has narrow path)

20 Turn L, then after S bend turn R – 50 m (55 yd) before sharp corner. Track turns L then R along field edge to full gate. **Take care** down rutted track to gate, then turn L across stone bridge up to farm

21 SA down to ford and into Mitford. Turn L onto B6343 to return to the start

19 Through bridle gate and turn L to bridleway marker post. Turn R to a bridle bridge at end of wood. **NB** slight depression is a 'holloway' denoting an old packhorse route. Follow this, keeping wood on your right, then on to minor road

The Rothbury Round

Rothbury is almost totally surrounded by heather-clad moors and wooded hills. Apart from one section of forest track this long ride offers non-stop panoramic views of the route. Starting at Rothbury, the ride climbs steadily to Simonside Forest. The long descent into Harwood Forest is followed by a gentle gradient to a wonderful view-point after which lies one of the most thrilling downhills in the UK! The short cut to Rothbury is via quiet minor roads and crosses the River Coquet beyond Newtown. If time and energy allow then continue north and tackle the steady ascent to Wreighill and enjoy the subsequent descent to the level riverside fields. The route then uses undulating field paths and deserted, minor roads and, after a steady climb, the uniformally graded Carriage Drive (track). The ensuing descent into Rothbury is as memorable as it is steep. NB Contact Forest Enterprise (Rothbury 01669 620569) for free permit to cycle in Forest Enterprise forests.

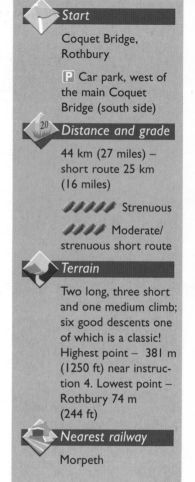

Start

Coquet Bridge, Rothbury

[P] Car park, west of the main Coquet Bridge (south side)

Distance and grade

44 km (27 miles) – short route 25 km (16 miles)

///// Strenuous

//// Moderate/ strenuous short route

Terrain

Two long, three short and one medium climb; six good descents one of which is a classic! Highest point – 381 m (1250 ft) near instruction 4. Lowest point – Rothbury 74 m (244 ft)

Nearest railway

Morpeth

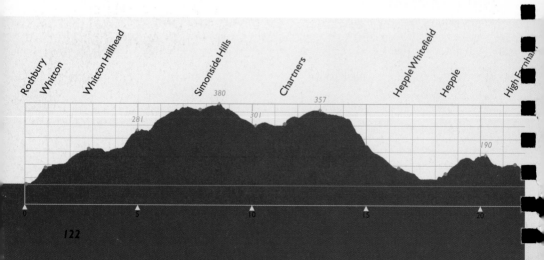

Places of interest

Cragside 1

A Victorian mansion built by the first Lord Armstrong in Wagnerian style – this showcase of Victorian art, architecture and technology is now a National Trust property. Set in 405 ha (1000 acres) of pine-covered hillside, lakes and tumbling streams, Cragside is especially famous for being the first (hydro) electrically powered house in the world. There are many other interesting features and remarkable inventions, too numerous to mention, all of which make Cragside a very special place

Holystone 8

Little more than a picturesque hamlet, Holystone offers an ideal *sojourn* on this major ride. The Salmon Inn has an old stone fireplace behind which is a hidden cavity for hiding smuggled goods. Holystone boasts two holy wells called St Mungo's and St Ninian's or the Lady's Well. Not far away, on Dove Crag Burn, lies Rob Roy's Cave

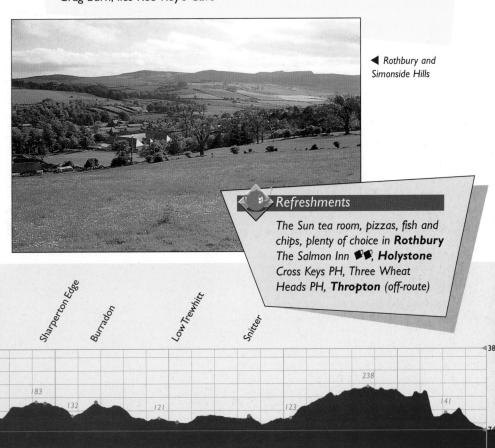

◀ Rothbury and Simonside Hills

Refreshments

The Sun tea room, pizzas, fish and chips, plenty of choice in **Rothbury** *The Salmon Inn* 🍴, **Holystone** *Cross Keys PH, Three Wheat Heads PH,* **Thropton** *(off-route)*

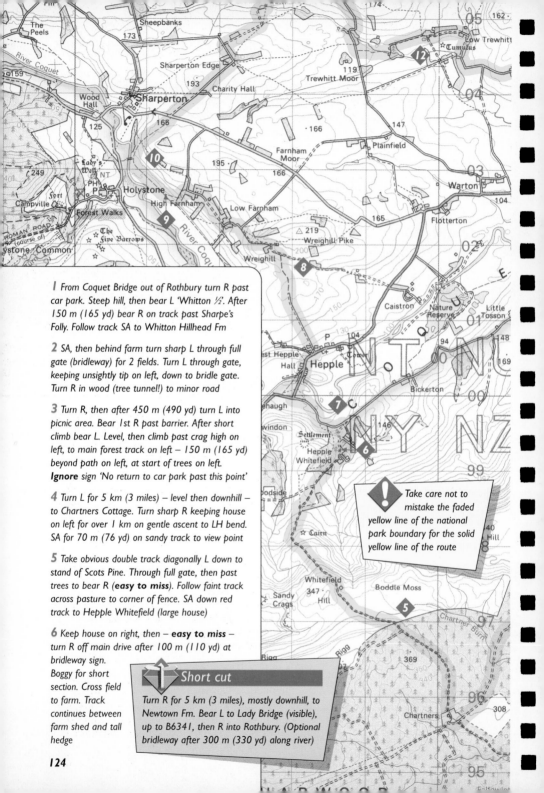

1 From Coquet Bridge out of Rothbury turn R past car park. Steep hill, then bear L 'Whitton ½'. After 150 m (165 yd) bear R on track past Sharpe's Folly. Follow track SA to Whitton Hillhead Fm

2 SA, then behind farm turn sharp L through full gate (bridleway) for 2 fields. Turn L through gate, keeping unsightly tip on left, down to bridle gate. Turn R in wood (tree tunnel!) to minor road

3 Turn R, then after 450 m (490 yd) turn L into picnic area. Bear 1st R past barrier. After short climb bear L. Level, then climb past crag high on left, to main forest track on left – 150 m (165 yd) beyond path on left, at start of trees on left. *Ignore* sign 'No return to car park past this point'

4 Turn L for 5 km (3 miles) – level then downhill – to Chartners Cottage. Turn sharp R keeping house on left for over 1 km on gentle ascent to LH bend. SA for 70 m (76 yd) on sandy track to view point

5 Take obvious double track diagonally L down to stand of Scots Pine. Through full gate, then past trees to bear R (**easy to miss**). Follow faint track across pasture to corner of fence. SA down red track to Hepple Whitefield (large house)

6 Keep house on right, then – **easy to miss** – turn R off main drive after 100 m (110 yd) at bridleway sign. Boggy for short section. Cross field to farm. Track continues between farm shed and tall hedge

> ⚠ Take care not to mistake the faded yellow line of the national park boundary for the solid yellow line of the route

⬆ Short cut

Turn R for 5 km (3 miles), mostly downhill, to Newtown Fm. Bear L to Lady Bridge (visible), up to B6341, then R into Rothbury. (Optional bridleway after 300 m (330 yd) along river)

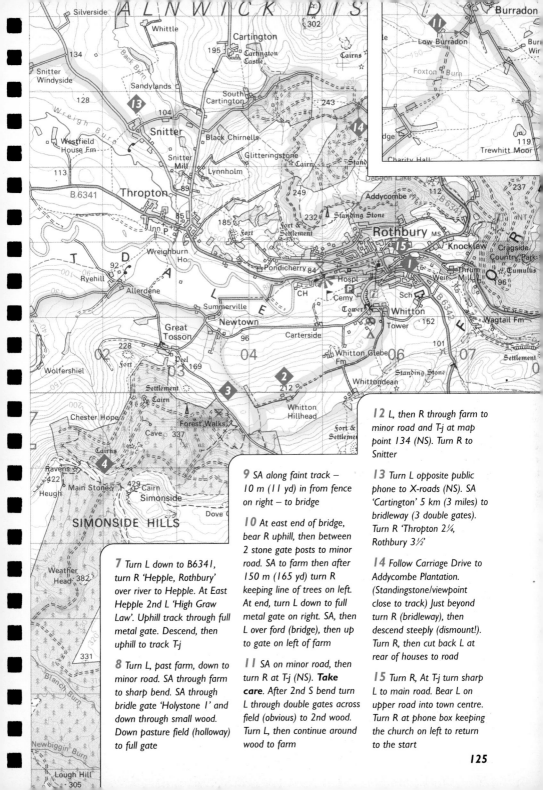

7 Turn L down to B6341, turn R 'Hepple, Rothbury' over river to Hepple. At East Hepple 2nd L 'High Graw Law'. Uphill track through full metal gate. Descend, then uphill to track T-j

8 Turn L, past farm, down to minor road. SA through farm to sharp bend. SA through bridle gate 'Holystone 1' and down through small wood. Down pasture field (holloway) to full gate

9 SA along faint track – 10 m (11 yd) in from fence on right – to bridge

10 At east end of bridge, bear R uphill, then between 2 stone gate posts to minor road. SA to farm then after 150 m (165 yd) turn R keeping line of trees on left. At end, turn L down to full metal gate on right. SA, then L over ford (bridge), then up to gate on left of farm

11 SA on minor road, then turn R at T-j (NS). **Take care**. After 2nd S bend turn L through double gates across field (obvious) to 2nd wood. Turn L, then continue around wood to farm

12 L, then R through farm to minor road and T-j at map point 134 (NS). Turn R to Snitter

13 Turn L opposite public phone to X-roads (NS). SA 'Cartington' 5 km (3 miles) to bridleway (3 double gates). Turn R 'Thropton 2¼, Rothbury 3½'

14 Follow Carriage Drive to Addycombe Plantation. (Standingstone/viewpoint close to track) Just beyond turn R (bridleway), then descend steeply (dismount!). Turn R, then cut back L at rear of houses to road

15 Turn R, At T-j turn sharp L to main road. Bear L on upper road into town centre. Turn R at phone box keeping the church on left to return to the start

125

1 South of Alnwick to the coast as far as Warkworth

The Northumbrian coastline is one of the finest in Britain. It is clean, sandy, continuous and interspersed with cliffs, quiet bays, hidden coves and rocky headlands and there are long stretches of sand dunes. But that is not all; there are many old seaports and tiny harbours – each with their own small fishing fleet. Then there are the castles of all sizes and states of repair and a diverse range of wildlife that the delicate coastline eco-structure supports. Cycling is an ideal way to enjoy the coast provided the routes and their surfaces are sustainable; by the year 2000 Sustrans' Coast & Castles Route will connect Berwick-upon-Tweed with Tynemouth for such a route. This ride, as with all of the coastal rides, takes in an area of coastal hinterland in order to make a circuit possible. Beginning at Alnwick, and heading seaward by railway paths, UCRs and quiet lanes, the bridleway along the dunes south of Alnmouth is used to reach the attractive town of Warkworth with its imposing castle and quaint market place. The return to Alnwick utilises a similar combination of hitherto little-used byways and quiet lanes which together make this ride a very enjoyable cycle tour.

Start

Outside of Alnwick just off the A1068 (GR 204125)

P Cross the A1, then turn down R into cul-de-sac

Distance and grade

43 km (27 miles) – short route 32 km (20 miles)

Easy

Terrain

Railway paths; edge of the sea bridleway; narrow lanes and green roads. Highest point – Freemans Hill 191 m (627 ft). Lowest point – sea level

Nearest railway

Alnmouth, just off the route near instructions 2/3

Alnwick | Greenrigg | High Buston | Birling Carrs | Warkworth | Warkworth Moor | Sturton Grange

107
39
60
2

0   5   10   15   20

The River Coquet approaching Warkworth

Close to yet another set of tight meanders with wooded cliffs stands Morwick Hall, formerly a property of the Grays of Howick. An old road passes by the Hall and goes down to one of two ancient fords, the lower one still known locally as Paupersford. When the river was safe to ford the grass lane which leads up to instruction 7 would have been the continuation route. When riding section 6, look out for the raised 'road' base which runs parallel to the hedge and meets this bridleway at right angles. From this traverse, a tall sandstone cliff catches the eye, on it are several ancient 'cup and ring' markings the purpose of which are not fully understood. These also occur elsewhere in Northumberland but none so close to sea level

▼ Alnmouth

Refreshments

Plenty of choice in **Alnwick**
Plenty of choice in **Warkworth**
The Cook and Barker Inn PH, **Newton on the Moor**
(off the route, via minor roads with dangerous A1 crossing)

Hazon

A1

Shiel Dykes

Hadwin's Close

Rugley Wood

122

164

191

25   30   35   40   43.0

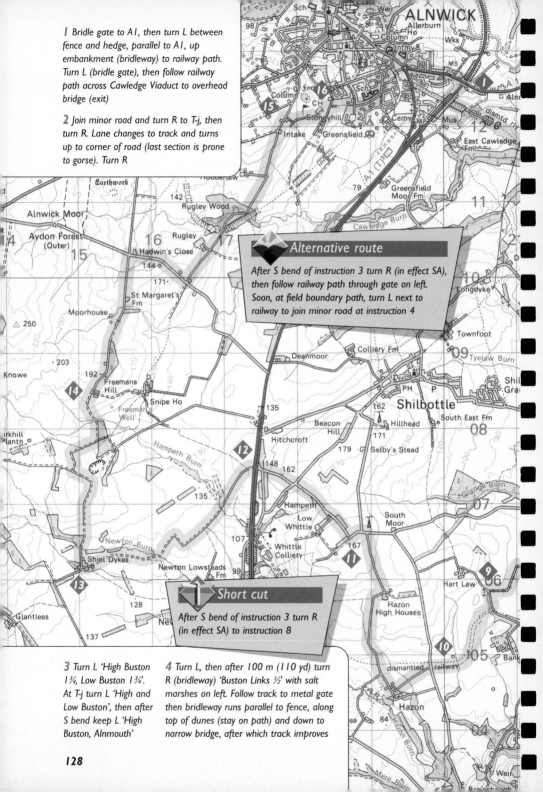

1 Bridle gate to A1, then turn L between fence and hedge, parallel to A1, up embankment (bridleway) to railway path. Turn L (bridle gate), then follow railway path across Cawledge Viaduct to overhead bridge (exit)

2 Join minor road and turn R to T-j, then turn R. Lane changes to track and turns up to corner of road (last section is prone to gorse). Turn R

Alternative route

After S bend of instruction 3 turn R (in effect SA), then follow railway path through gate on left. Soon, at field boundary path, turn L next to railway to join minor road at instruction 4

Short cut

After S bend of instruction 3 turn R (in effect SA) to instruction 8

3 Turn L 'High Buston 1¾, Low Buston 1¾'. At T-j turn L 'High and Low Buston', then after S bend keep L 'High Buston, Alnmouth'

4 Turn L, then after 100 m (110 yd) turn R (bridleway) 'Buston Links ½' with salt marshes on left. Follow track to metal gate then bridleway runs parallel to fence, along top of dunes (stay on path) and down to narrow bridge, after which track improves

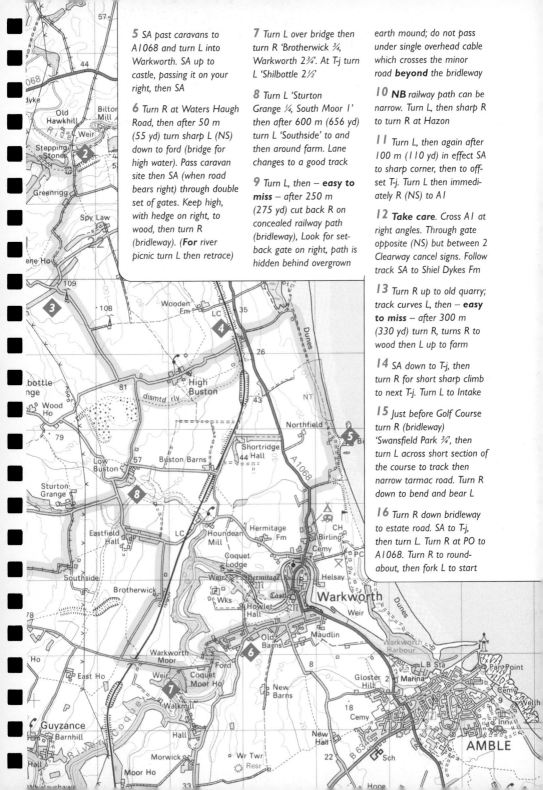

5 SA past caravans to A1068 and turn L into Warkworth. SA up to castle, passing it on your right, then SA

6 Turn R at Waters Haugh Road, then after 50 m (55 yd) turn sharp L (NS) down to ford (bridge for high water). Pass caravan site then SA (when road bears right) through double set of gates. Keep high, with hedge on right, to wood, then turn R (bridleway). (**For** river picnic turn L then retrace)

7 Turn L over bridge then turn R 'Brotherwick ¾, Warkworth 2¾'. At T-j turn L 'Shilbottle 2½'

8 Turn L 'Sturton Grange ¼, South Moor 1' then after 600 m (656 yd) turn L 'Southside' to and then around farm. Lane changes to a good track

9 Turn L, then – **easy to miss** – after 250 m (275 yd) cut back R on concealed railway path (bridleway), Look for set-back gate on right, path is hidden behind overgrown

earth mound; do not pass under single overhead cable which crosses the minor road **beyond** the bridleway

10 **NB** railway path can be narrow. Turn L, then sharp R to turn R at Hazon

11 Turn L, then again after 100 m (110 yd) in effect SA to sharp corner, then to off-set T-j. Turn L then immediately R (NS) to A1

12 **Take care**. Cross A1 at right angles. Through gate opposite (NS) but between 2 Clearway cancel signs. Follow track SA to Shiel Dykes Fm

13 Turn R up to old quarry; track curves L, then – **easy to miss** – after 300 m (330 yd) turn R, turns R to wood then L up to farm

14 SA down to T-j, then turn R for short sharp climb to next T-j. Turn L to Intake

15 Just before Golf Course turn R (bridleway) 'Swansfield Park ¾', then turn L across short section of the course to track then narrow tarmac road. Turn R down to bend and bear L

16 Turn R down bridleway to estate road. SA to T-j, then turn L. Turn R at PO to A1068. Turn R to round-about, then fork L to start

8 East of Alnwick to the coast, north to Craster

Start

Next to B1340, north of Alnwick, before slip road to A1 (GR 200143)

P As above

Distance and grade

34 km (21 miles) – short route 32 km (20 miles)

Easy/moderate

Easy

Terrain

Green roads, quiet lanes and bridleways – mostly level. Highest point – between instructions 14/15 105 m (344 ft). Lowest point – sea level

Nearest railway

Alnmouth, on the route

This ride has the benefit of including a reasonable length of coastal cycling, again part of the Sustrans' Coast & Castles Route. Using a different route out of Alnwick, the River Aln is forded (once wet, the already tricky stepping stones are lethal) after which there is a brief overlap with off-road Route 7 – offering an alternative approach when the river is likely to be high. Then it is down to Alnmouth before an unavoidable on-road stretch to Boulmer and the start of a first class cliff-top track to Sea Houses. There is a short on-road link up to a contrasting rural section then it is down the road to Craster with its tiny harbour and seaside cottages. Looping back through Dunstan, two almost-connecting off-road sections lead through the sleepy village of Rennington to 4 km (2½ miles) of UCR leaving a little over 2 km (1¼ miles) of relatively quiet B road which gently slopes back to the start.

Refreshments

Plenty of choice in **Alnwick**
Plenty of choice in **Alnmouth**
Jolly Fisherman PH, Bark Pots tea room, shop and restaurant, **Craster**
Cottage Inn PH, **Dunstan**
Horse Shoes Inn PH, **Rennington**

The coast

Boulmer lifeboat station stands next to the road and is indicative of the skill and courage that this important service exemplifies. There are always a number of cobles nearby; these are Northumbrian fishing boats based on an original design concept borrowed from the Viking long boats which allows the boats to be launched from the beach and still be very stable on the sea in all conditions. Note the guide posts in the bay which indicate a safe channel for the boats. Houdiemont Sands and Sugar Sands are two lovely beaches as is Howick Haven; Rumbling Kern is a cave which causes the sea to growl when it swells into it at certain tide levels and strengths, colloquially called a 'woofy hole' which is onomatopoeic!

▼ *Craster*

Howick Hall — Dunstan — Littlemill — Rennington — Broxfield — Denwick Lane End

47

105

20 25 30 33.8

1 *Cross A1, then turn R at Denwick church, tarmac changes to track (Rabbit Lonnen)* **NB** *'Lonnen' means a lane. At A1068 turn L, then next R at X-roads to river –* **take care** *– stepping stones are very slippery and uneven do not attempt to cross if they are submerged! If uncertain, return to A1068 and turn L to follow instruction 1 of off-road Route 7*

2 *Up to Greenrigg Fm, turn left to Bilton. Turn L to Hipsburn roundabout then SA to Alnmouth roundabout. Turn R for Main Street and at far end turn L to loop back to instruction 3*

3 *SA keeping church on your L to fork, then turn R to Boulmer – a necessary on-road section*

4 *SA at sharp corner (2 cul-de-sac signs) along cliff track for 3 km (2 miles) and enjoy this fine coastal path*

5 *Turn L to Howick Hall entrance*

6 *Turn R past wall on your left, then SA to follow high deer fence on your left, through gate with mature wood on your left to far end. Turn L through gate on your left (**ignore** gate SA into open field), then after 10 m (11 yd), almost into next field, bear R –* **easy to miss** *– along narrow path through narrow belt of mature trees*

7 *Turn L on good track for 200 m (220 yd) then at bend turn R along field edge keeping plantation on your right (2 fields). Cross small bridge, then through bridle gate and turn L along field edge to corner of field. Turn R along field edge to road*

Short cut

Turn L down to instruction 11

8 *Turn R to X-roads. Turn L to Dunstan (PH) then bear L to next bend in road (**Or** SA to Craster/Dunstanburgh Castle then retrace to Dunstan Village)*

9 *Through bridle gate, past old hemmel (stone, cattle building), follow edge of field (bridleway) keeping wood and fence on your left, to next wood. Through gate, then turn L down tree avenue. Next section to bridle gate is uneven due to horse use and muddy when wet – walk if necessary*

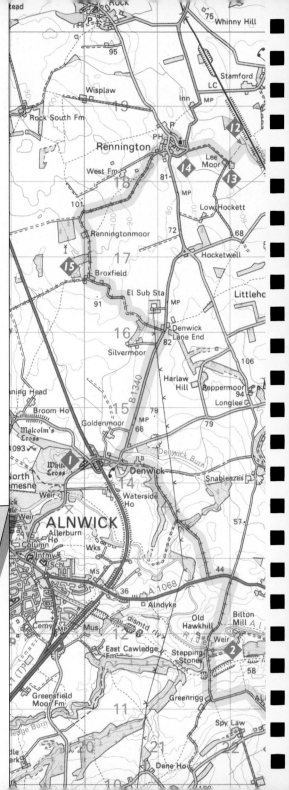

10 SA along field edge keeping fence and both blocks of trees on your left, through gate, then SA on obvious double track to minor road. Turn L

11 Turn R (field gate some 100 m (110 yd) NW of small bridge before X-roads) and follow field edge next to fence on your right. Through tunnel, then turn R (best line is some 10 m (11 yd) in from railway fence)

12 *Easy to miss*. Turn L to bridle gate (between 4th/5th railway pylons from tunnel and some 120 m (130 yd) before single wooden electric power pole in field). Cross small bridge. **NB** Conservation notice through gate on left. You are now on a Countryside Access farm; SA with fence on your left

13 Turn R at farm and cross open area. SA passing cottages on your left (sign 'Farm Walk' – please show considera-tion). Through end gate, then bear L towards church keeping hedge on your left

14 Turn R, then L (in effect SA) 'Rock 1¼' into Rennington (PH). Turn L, then turn R at end of village green at farm. After 200 m (220 yd), at end of cottages, fork L

15 *Take care*. Through farm, then turn L to B1340 and turn R to return to the start

A super circuit on scenic byways, south of Wooler

The rolling Cheviot Hills are full of wild places (they have an indigenous herd of wild goats) and it is not difficult to feel lonely when cycling or walking in their midst – or even in their mist! This ride comes within gasping distance of these wonderful hills and through proximity provides a taste of what they have to offer the committed off-road cyclist. Our route heads south of Wooler along narrow, minor roads and old byways that were once the area's main thoroughfares. After several enjoyable undulations the rewarding descent into Roseden is capped with a high-quality refreshment opportunity before the route swings very pleasantly eastwards towards Old Bewick. The ascent and subsequent cross-fell section take you to the aptly named Blawearie. A surprisingly acceptable fell track links with the magnificent Hepburn Moor road (see on-road Route 12) and with the further use of quiet lanes and green roads the return route to Wooler maintains its interest and charm with more bountiful views of the Cheviots.

 Start

High Street, Wooler

P Padgepool Place to the west of Wooler High Street

Distance and grade

34 km (21 miles) – short route 20 km (12 miles)

Moderate

 Terrain

Descents seem to outweigh the ascents over this mixed terrain route. The Hepburn downhill is amazing but needs control and traffic awareness. Highest point – fell approaching instruction 7 253 m (830 ft). Lowest point – near Wooler 52 m (172 ft).

Nearest railway

Berwick-upon-Tweed, 28 km (17 miles) north of Wooler

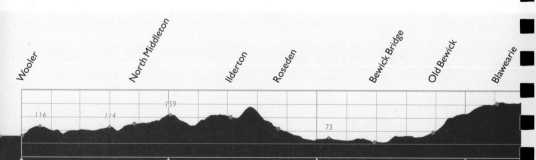

Wooler 1

Wooler means 'hill overlooking a stream' and makes the ideal base for an extended visit to this area and one which gives easy access to the Cheviot Hills. Situated on a small plateau and its approach slopes, the small market town of Wooler overlooks the Wooler Water. Passing by such evocative places as Scald Hill, Skirl Naked and Happy Valley, the Wooler Water is then deflected northwards to its confluence with the River Till which then kinks its way north westwards with the sole purpose of emptying its contents into the River Tweed

The Cheviot Hills

The Cheviot Hills stretch for about 35 km (22 miles) along the northwest border of Northumberland and being some 32 km (21 miles) wide, the total area of rolling, grassy and heather-clad hills, of which about one third lies in Scotland, amounts to over 777 km^2 (300 miles^2) of wonderful scenery

The Bewicks

Bewick means 'bee farm' which bears testimony to the fact that the neighbouring moors are a reliable source of honey. In times gone by, this was of great significance before imported sugar became available and honey was virtually the only source of available sweetening and beeswax was used in great quantities both in the home and in churches. The left turn to tiny Old Bewick church, next to the Kirk Burn, is marked by an inscribed Saxon cross and is well worth the slight detour – it is said to have been built by Queen Maud, wife of Henry I. Ancient earthworks abound as do cup and ring marked rocks. En route to Blawearie an old wagonway lies next to several holloways, where rock has been chiselled to permit wheeled passage

◆ Refreshments

Plenty of choice in **Wooler**
Tea room, restaurant and shop,
Roseden Farm

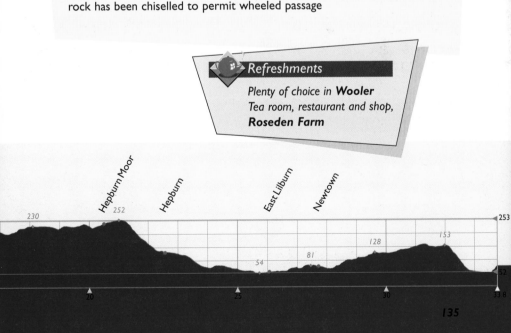

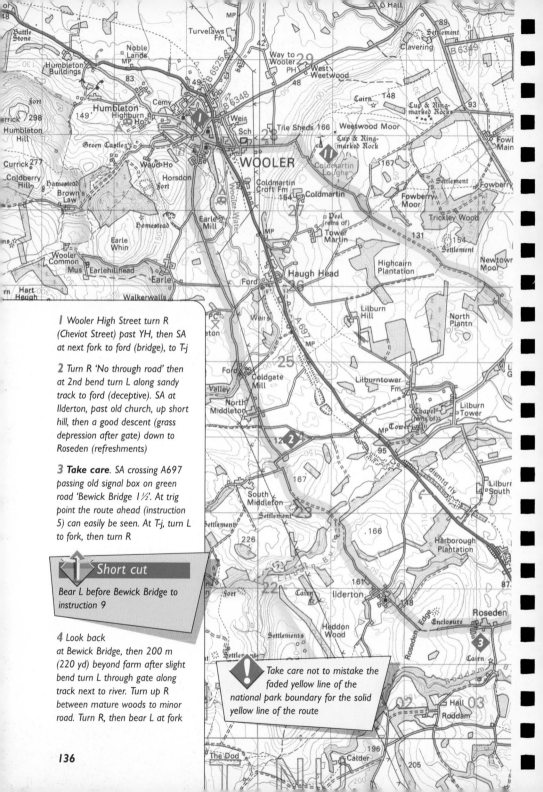

1 Wooler High Street turn R (Cheviot Street) past YH, then SA at next fork to ford (bridge), to T-j

2 Turn R 'No through road' then at 2nd bend turn L along sandy track to ford (deceptive). SA at Ilderton, past old church, up short hill, then a good descent (grass depression after gate) down to Roseden (refreshments)

3 **Take care**. SA crossing A697 passing old signal box on green road 'Bewick Bridge 1½'. At trig point the route ahead (instruction 5) can easily be seen. At T-j, turn L to fork, then turn R

Short cut

Bear L before Bewick Bridge to instruction 9

4 Look back at Bewick Bridge, then 200 m (220 yd) beyond farm after slight bend turn L through gate along track next to river. Turn up R between mature woods to minor road. Turn R, then bear L at fork

! Take care not to mistake the faded yellow line of the national park boundary for the solid yellow line of the route

5 Turn L at farm and follow track ahead up to fell. Through metal gate, then bear L to distant gate. Track reduces up to Blawearie. *Warning* – do not continue in bad visibility or inclement weather. (Navigation aid: if visible/after Blawearie – head to distant mast on right)

6 Stay a while to enjoy this wonderful place! Follow track behind and beyond Blawearie, short climb before descent to track T-j 30 m (33 yd) in front of sheep cabin. Turn R across seemingly open fell and follow track close to holloways. Look for a marker post, a hurdle gate close to small

stream, 2 further marker posts then track improves to road

7 Turn L across moor (narrow road), then descend carefully down 1:8 hill (exceptional views) to T-j. SA down grass lane. *Warning* – do not attempt instruction 8 if the river is likely to be full. If uncertain, advance inspection is recommended (short detour before instruction 4)

8 Turn L down to river (footbridge unusable) which can be crossed by stepping-stones (homemade) or paddling (through hurdle on R, then across to shingle shore), then on to minor road

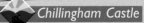

Chillingham Castle

Turn R to Chillingham Castle gates, then turn L to Newtown T-j. Turn R to continue with instruction 10

9 Turn R to farm T-j and turn R over ford (bridge) to Newtown T-j

10 Bear L to wide junction then SA 'West Lilburn'. Lane changes to track, keep SA

11 Track changes to tarmac lane, descend steeply – *take care* – to cross A697 and up the short, sharp sting in the tail to return to the start

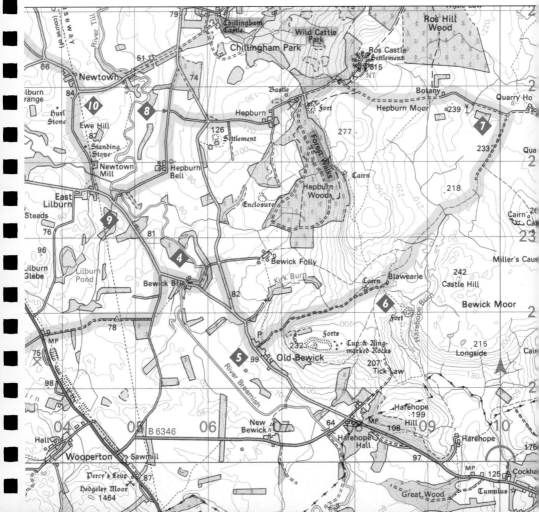

West of Belford to St Cuthbert's Cave and Ravens Crag

Fractionally the shortest ride in the book (more so if you take the short cut). This ride is recommended for its special qualities; take a generous measure of situation and add incredible views on all sides, plenty of history and atmosphere with wildlife habitats and wetlands, add some favourable gradients and this ride is the result! Starting at Belford, what was possibly an old thoroughfare or through route, heads northwest past a variety of interesting locations, to the Swinhoe road. Passing the old continuation road on the right an excellent track slopes up gently to Dick's Oldwalls and then girdles the hill past eye-catching Cockenheugh and the splendid St Cuthbert's Cave. After traversing close to Holburn Farm, a short climb curves round Raven's Crag and past Holburn Moss to descend pleasantly to Detchant. The A1 crossing needs great care and after a short woodland thrash, the return route loops back to Belford by a quiet, minor road which only becomes busier in the final 2 km (1¼ miles). Choose a fine day and enjoy this lovely circuit – it may be short but it contains more than its fair share of magic.

Start

Main Street, Belford

P On B6349 west end of Belford

Distance and grade

21 km (13 miles) – short route 18 km (11 miles)

Easy

Terrain

Despite the comparative brevity of this route, it contains within it a wide range of ground surfaces although principally the route follows good tracks. Some sections can be muddy after rain or overgrown in mid summer. Highest point – Holburn Moss 160 m (525 ft). Lowest point – near Elwick 5 m (17 ft)

Nearest railway

Berwick-upon-Tweed, 24 km (15 miles) north of the start

Belford

Swinhoe Farm

156

147

Raven's Crag

151

95

0

5

10

St Cuthbert's Cave 5

This remarkable natural sandstone cave is where, it is thought, the saint's body rested for a short time on its way to Durham. In 1833, a medieval ring was found in this cave, one of a number of such finds in the locality. A visit in springtime is rewarded with an avenue of daffodils which lead the eye down through the wider avenue of pines to where the not-so-distant Cheviot Hills are perfectly framed

Holburn Moss 6

Holburn Moss is one of only two Ramsar sites in the North East of England, the other being on Holy Island; representing over 90 countries, the Ramsar Convention, named after the town in Iran, exists to conserve important wetland sites

Smeafield 9

Originally Smith's Field, but the type of field all depends on the date of the name; prior to the Black Death in 1348, the word 'feld' meant an open space or expanse larger than a clearing as in Flodden Field. Land enclosure after the Black Death saw the gradual adoption of 'field' as we now know it

◀ St Cuthbert's Cave near Belford in Glendale

153   Greymare Farm   Detchant Lodge   Elwick   160

15   6   20   21.4

1 W from Main Street on B6349, turn R at Community Club (bridleway) to Westhall Fm, then turn R at steading to Craggyhall Fm. SA past old lime kiln to gate. Follow field-edge path to bridle gate

2 Through gate into wood (permissive path) to track T-j (white house ahead). Turn L to minor road, then SA to Swinhoe Fm

Short cut

Just before farm, turn R through belt of trees, through gate and along raised field-edge path (fence on right) to gate. Through gate, turn R and follow improving track to minor road

3 SA past farm on wide track past Dick Oldwalls (disused building) and on to trees (coastal views to rear)

4 SA, then track bears R and with trees only on your right, good views of the Cheviots. Look for Cockenheugh rock towers on your R followed by St Cuthbert's Cave on your R near end of wood

5 SA to contour hillside and on to lane east of Holburn Fm. Look out for field edge dogs leg L, then R 400 m (¼ mile) before farm track

6 Turn R, then uphill to circuit between Raven's Crag and Rabbit Hill re-entering trees. Follow obvious track out of trees, around and down, to Greymare Fm

7 SA by farm to minor road, then down to Detchant (short-cut track comes in from right). SA to Detchant Lodge

8 **Take great care.** SA on track to cross A1, then SA over railway line into belt of tall trees down to cross small bridge. Track then turns R up to minor road (long grass in Summer)

9 Turn R, then at obvious fork bear R

10 Turn R, then over LC on busier road. Cross A1 – **take care** – using offset tarmac footpaths for increased safety then SA back to Start

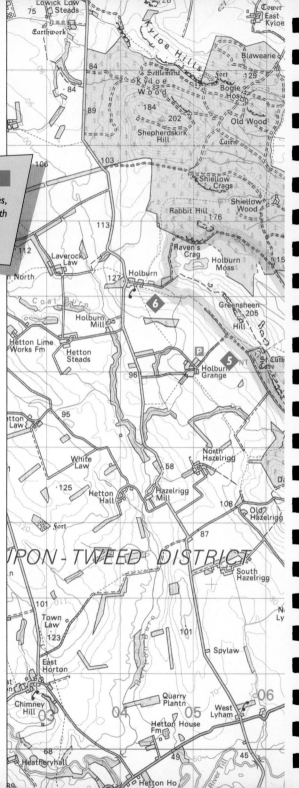

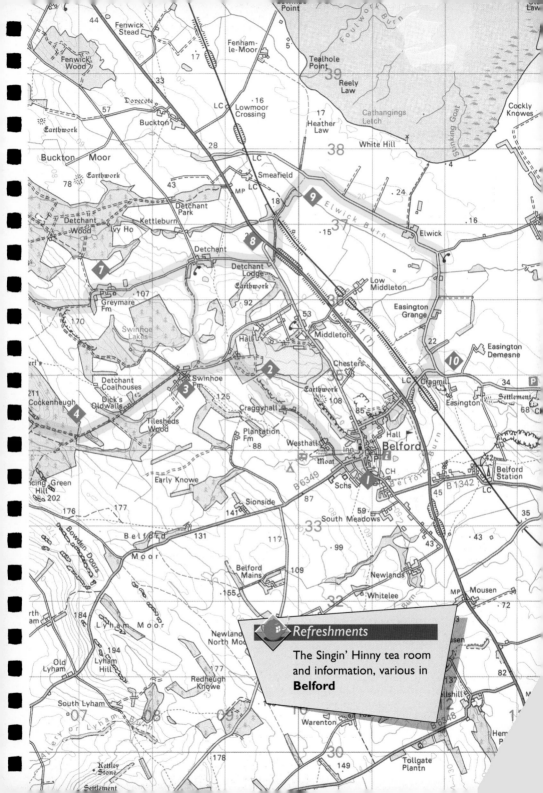

Refreshments

The Singin' Hinny tea room and information, various in **Belford**

Cycle Cycle Cycle
TOURS TOURS TOURS

The Ordnance Survey Cycle Tours series

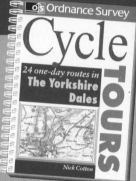

- ◆ Around Birmingham
- ◆ Around London
- ◆ Avon, Somerset & Wiltshire
- ◆ Berks, Bucks & Oxfordshire
- ◆ Central Scotland
- ◆ Cornwall & Devon
- ◆ Cumbria & the Lakes
- ◆ Dorset, Hampshire & Isle of Wight
- ◆ East Anglia – South
- ◆ Gloucestershire and Hereford & Worcester
- ◆ Kent, Surrey & Sussex
- ◆ North Wales and The Marches
- ◆ North Yorkshire & Teesside
- ◆ Northumberland and County Durham
- ◆ Peak District
- ◆ Southern Scotland
- ◆ South, West and Mid-Wales
- ◆ Yorkshire Dales

*T*he whole series is available from all good bookshops or by mail order direct from the publisher. Payment can be made by credit card or cheque/postal order in the following ways:

By phone Phone your order through on our special *Credit Card Hotline* on *01733 371999 (Fax: 01733 370585)*. Speak to our customer service team during office hours (9am to 5pm) or leave a message on the answer machine, quoting your full credit card number plus expiry date and your full name and address and reference.

Simply fill out the order form (you may photcopy it) and send it to: *Reed Direct, 43 Stapledon Road, Orton Southgate, Peterborough PE2 6TD.*

Ordnance Survey Cycle TOURS ORDER FORM

I wish to order the following titles	Quantity @ £9.99 each	£ Total
AROUND BIRMINGHAM	☐ 0 600 58623 5 ➤	
AROUND LONDON	☐ 0 600 58845 9 ➤	
AVON, SOMERSET & WILTSHIRE	☐ 0 600 58664 2 ➤	
BERKS, BUCKS & OXFORDSHIRE	☐ 0 600 58156 X ➤	
CENTRAL SCOTLAND	☐ 0 600 59005 4 ➤	
CORNWALL & DEVON	☐ 0 600 58124 1 ➤	
CUMBRIA & THE LAKES	☐ 0 600 58126 8 ➤	
DORSET, HAMPSHIRE & ISLE OF WIGHT	☐ 0 600 58667 7 ➤	
EAST ANGLIA – SOUTH	☐ 0 600 58125 X ➤	
GLOUCESTERSHIRE AND HEREFORD & WORCESTER	☐ 0 600 58665 0 ➤	
KENT, SURREY & SUSSEX	☐ 0 600 58666 9 ➤	
NORTH WALES AND THE MARCHES	☐ 0 600 59007 0 ➤	
NORTH YORKSHIRE & TEESSIDE	☐ 0 600 59103 4 ➤	
NORTHUMBERLAND AND COUNTY DURHAM	☐ 0 600 59105 0 ➤	
PEAK DISTRICT	☐ 0 600 58889 0 ➤	
SOUTHERN SCOTLAND	☐ 0 600 58624 3 ➤	
SOUTH, WEST AND MID-WALES	☐ 0 600 58846 7 ➤	
YORKSHIRE DALES	☐ 0 600 58847 5 ➤	

Name..

Address..

....

....Postcode

◆ **Free postage and packing**

◆ All available titles will normally be dispatched within 5 working days of receipt of order but please allow up to 28 days for delivery

◆ Whilst every effort is made to keep prices low, the publisher reserves the right to increase prices at short notice

☐ Please tick this box if you do not wish your name to be used by other carefully selected organisations that may wish to send you information about other products and services

Registered Office: Michelin House, 81 Fulham Road, London SW3 6RB. Registered in England number 1974080

I enclose a cheque/postal order, for a **total** of ☐

made payable to *Reed Book Services*, or please debit my

☐ Access ☐ American Express ☐ Visa ☐ Diners

account by ☐

Account no

☐☐☐☐ ☐☐☐☐ ☐☐☐☐ ☐☐☐☐

Expiry date ☐☐ ☐☐

Signature...

Post to: Reed Books Direct, 43 Stapledon Road, Orton Southgate, Peterborough PE2 6TD